PENDULUM
Workbook

PENDULUM
Workbook

Markus Schirner

Sterling Publishing Co., Inc.
New York

Library of Congress Cataloging-in-Publication Data

Schirner, Markus.

  [Pendel-Welten. English]

  Pendulum workbook / Markus Schirner.

     p.   cm.

  Includes index.

  ISBN 0-8069-5731-X

  Fortune-telling by pendulum. I. Title.

BF1779.P45S3513 1999

133.3'23dc21   98-33188

                                                    CIP

Be sure to consult your doctor before taking any oils, herbs, or other charted substances internally.

Background art courtesy of Corel Draw

1 3 5 7 9 10 8 6 4 2

Published by Sterling Publishing Company, Inc.

387 Park Avenue South, New York, N.Y. 10016

English translation copyright

©1999 by Sterling Publishing Company, Inc.

Originally published in Germany as *Pendel-Welten* ©1995 by Schirner Verlag, Darmstadt, Germany

Distributed in Canada by Sterling Publishing

c/o Canadian Manda Group, One Atlantic Avenue, Suite 105 Toronto, Ontario, Canada M6K 3E7

Distributed in Great Britain and Europe by Cassell PLC

Wellington House, 125 Strand, London WC2R OBB, England

Distributed in Australia by Capricorn Link (Australia) Pty Ltd.

P.O. Box 6651, Baulkham Hills, Business Centre, NSW 2153, Australia

Printed and Bound in Hong Kong

Sterling ISBN 0-8069-5731-X

Contents

The Pendulum Charts

Preface

The results you get with a pendulum depend upon your special sensitivity to the invisible rays, vibrations, sensations, and impressions that you can perceive with the help of a pendulum. You can interpret them and evaluate them according to certain principles and methods that you will learn here.

The pendulum is an amplifier; it brings your own perceptions into visible form. When you use the pendulum you are both sender and receiver, with the capability of feeling rays -- a capability that all living creatures (humans, animals, and plants) share.

Many books have been written about pendulums, but practical instructions are rare. Keep in mind that mastering the pendulum is an art, but applying it consciously is a science.

In this spirit, the authors, the graphic designers, the editors, and the publishing company wish you lots of success. The motto of this book is "Practice makes the Master."

Introduction

This book supplies practical material that makes working with the pendulum easier. The instructions are brief and to the point. Instead of long-winded explanations, you'll get precise visual commentaries. It's not the purpose of this book to enter deeply into the philosophy of swinging the pendulum, nor to explore the energies that are behind it. But, of course, that doesn't mean that you couldn't benefit from researching that in other pendulum books.

General Issues

Everyone is basically capable of working with the pendulum. Only a few situations can diminish this capability. So, here are two important points to start with:

1. You need practice, practice, practice. As in school, you start with the first step and become expert through constant practice and experiment.

2. Mistakes are part of the learning process. No result is infallible. But if you don't use the pendulum for egoistic reasons, but only for the well being of others or yourself—and/or for spiritual growth—your results will become secure, clear, and reliable.

The only way to learn how to use the pendulum is through practical work. Proceed step by step and pay attention to the following basic ideas about this intriguing topic.

Basic Issues

1. The results you get with the pendulum reflect your stage of spiritual/mental development.

2. Increasing your sensitivity will enhance your pendulum work. The more perceptive you are toward your environment, the more receptive and precise your pendulum's results will be.

3. Dealing with other people and with fine substances -- as well as a connection with the higher worlds of the spirit -- require that you be free of egotism. Only swing the pendulum for the following reasons:

* to train your spirit
* out of a genuine desire for knowledge—only for the sake of the truth—or unselfishly, to help other people or other creatures.

4. Never act out of ego.

5. Never swing the pendulum for demonstration purposes in front of other people.

6. Never swing the pendulum into the future.

7. Always concentrate on the problem or the formulation of the question. Only when body and spirit are one can the pendulum show true results.

8. Always check your results. Never consider that the result you get is infallible.

9. Inner humility and gratitude, as well as a healthy respect for the cosmic forces you will come in touch with, should always be part of your pendulum work.

How to Deal Practically with the Pendulum

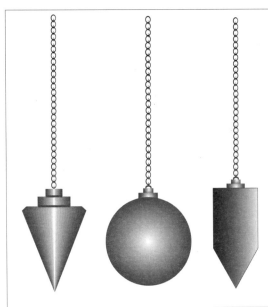

Which pendulum is best to use?

It's not a question of the best pendulum, but of the pendulum user! Never allow yourself to become dependent on a tool, because that would take away your freedom—and that lack of freedom could disturb your results. Follow your intuition when selecting your pendulum. Choose one that you like!

You can also make a pendulum yourself. Take a thread, a chain, or a hair and hang a weight on it. You can use a screw, a button, a cork, or any other object; it's up to you.

What are the first steps?

1. Hold the pendulum loosely, placing the upper end between your thumb and forefinger (see the illustration). The thread can range from 6 to 8 inches (15 to 20cm) long. It's a good idea to tie a knot in the thread at the length where the swing of the pendulum feels best.

2. Rest your elbow on the table and keep your hand hanging loosely from your wrist. Your fingers need to be loose, too.

3. Make sure your upper body and back are straight, so that your energy can flow freely.

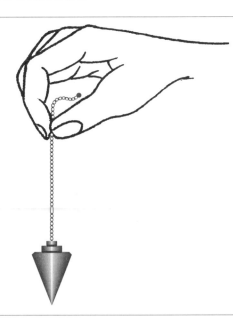

4. Let your feet make good contact with the floor (do not cross them).

5. Put your other hand flat on the table.

6. Relax. Let your breath flow calmly.

7. Do not let yourself be distracted by others in your environment—or by the TV or radio or other noise. Make sure before you start using the pendulum that you will be left alone.

8. Do not swing the pendulum when you're tired.

SWINGING THE PENDULUM REQUIRES THAT YOU BE UNDIVIDED AND TOTALLY PRESENT IN THE MOMENT.

First determine what each pendulum movement means for you. Ask your pendulum, "What does a YES look like?" After that, "What does a NO look like?"

Every pendulum movement is possible (see drawing at the right). Find out what yours mean. When you have determined a clear YES and NO, ask what its sign is for "I don't want to answer," or "I can't answer that."

It you have problems getting an answer or understanding the meaning of the swing, consciously *make* the pendulum swing and ask again: the pendulum's movement will be clearer. After practice, the force of the swing will increase.

You can also determine YES and NO beforehand. Generally, you can use the following principles:

Right turn = + = positive = YES
Left turn = – = negative = NO

Using the illustration below, hold your pendulum exactly over the center of the pendulum symbol that is drawn on it.

Basic Exercises

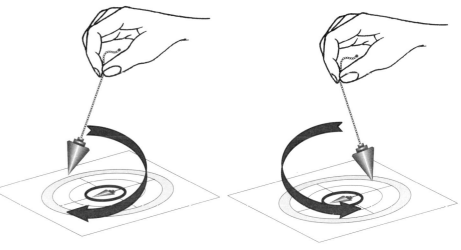

Right Turn

Left Turn

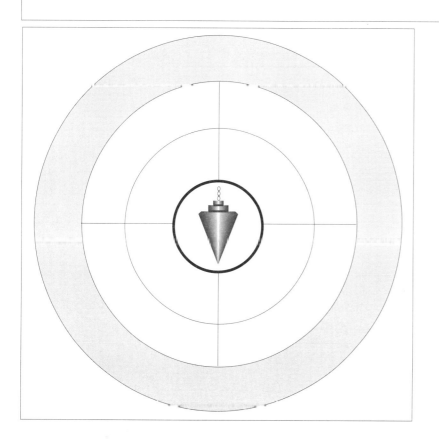

From front to back

From right to left

9

Once you have determined your YES and NO, don't deviate from it.

Practical Exercises for Getting to Know Your Pendulum

To check the capabilities of your pendulum, try these exercises:

1. Take two glasses, which, if possible, look the same and are the same shape. Fill them with tap water (the amount of water is not important). Place the glasses next to each other at a distance of about 16 inches (40cm), And hold the pendulum between them. Ask the pendulum whether the contents of the two glasses are the same.

Your pendulum may swing back and forth between the glasses. That would mean that YES, a correspondence—an analogy—exists!

If the pendulum does not move, concentrate anew on the question, and then wait patiently, until the pendulum's movement takes place—that is, until the contents of both glasses are recognized as identical by the pendulum (illus 1).

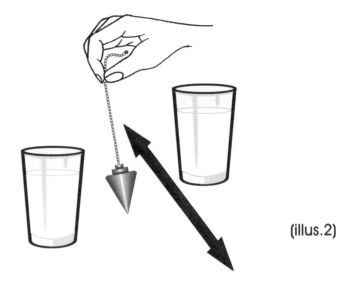

(illus.2)

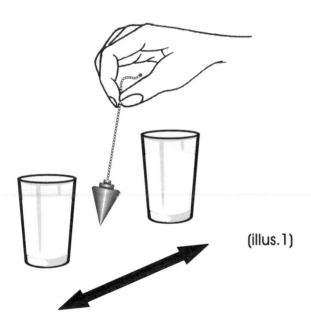

(illus.1)

Once you have mastered this task successfully, you need to continue to the next task:

2. Hold the pendulum between yourself and one of the glasses. Ask whether you should drink the water as it came out of the tap. If the pendulum moves between you and the glass in a back-and-forth swing, it means you've gotten a YES. Actually, in view of today's water quality, most of the time you may get a dividing line (illus 2.), which means that the pendulum has rejected it.

You can master this pendulum experiment easily. When you do, it is a sign that your pendulum techniques are working.

3. Now a last test we will do together, so that you can build up your confidence for the time when you're working with the charts.

Pour the water out of one of the two glasses. Dry the glass thoroughly and fill it with mineral water from a bottle. Now place the glasses about 16 inches (40cm) apart. Ask again whether the content of the two glasses is the same.

You will be surprised. Even though it is water in both cases, you will receive at best a diagonal movement of the pendulum, if not actually a dividing line. In the first case, it means that the water is somehow similar; in the second case, it means that the content of the two glasses is not comparable, for whatever reason.

You can repeat this exercise with other materials. For example, take two apples that come from different places, two kinds of soft drinks, and so on. There are no limits to the possibilities. When you do this test, keep in mind that you are examining a relationship between the two materials. This is called questioning resonance.

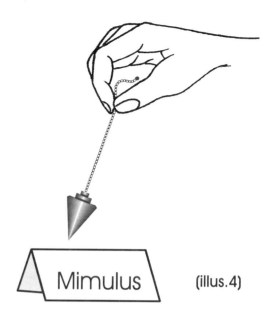

Mimulus (illus.4)

(illus.3)

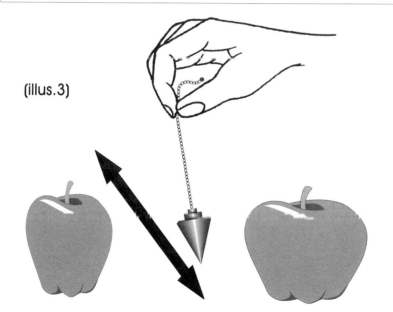

You can also do this test as we do it in the pages of this book—with words. For example, you can write the word "Mimulus" on a piece of paper (it's one of the Bach flowers), and with its help you can find out whether you need this flower essence for your mental well-being. If you do need it, the pendulum will turn to the right.

Of course, you can do this test with every one of the Bach flowers. You can also continue it with the names of trees. Ask, for example, whether the cedar is suitable for you, whether you should recharge your energy from this tree.

Or, here is another example: Copy down the names of one or two therapies that might be helpful to you; for example "Autogenous Training" and "Hapkido." Question the value of the therapy to you—with the pendulum and the written word.

The Testing of Objects

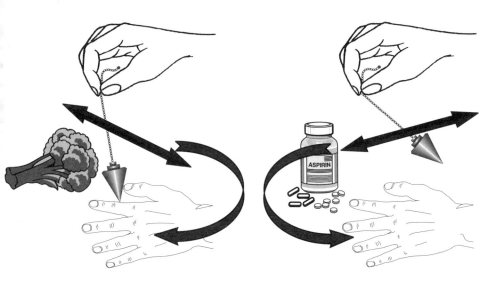

From the hand to the object
circle = positive

Between hand and object or right
or left circle = negative

Running alongside the hand
= positive

Running away from the hand
= negative

You can ask about anything you like with the pendulum, if the question can be answered with a YES or NO.

Of course, there are other ways to deal with the pendulum. The safest method is to swing it at the object itself. Whether you want to test your groceries, your medications, Bach flower remedies, or gemstones, there are no limits to what you can find out.

To use this method, place the object on the table, hold your hand next to the object at a distance of about 10 inches (25cm). Then take your pendulum and hold it between your hand and the object. Free yourself completely of any inner dialogue or unnecessary thoughts, and try to sense only the energy of the object lying next to you. The pendulum will swing back and forth either between the object and your hand (to the right), which will indicate a positive answer, or it will swing from the front to the back (left to right), which indicates a clear division—negative energy.

You can also hold your hand over an object and let the pendulum hang over the center of your hand (see illustration). If the pendulum swings in the direction of your hand (in the flowing energy of the body), then it indicates a positive answer. If it swings in a transverse motion to your hand, then the energy between the object and you is negative.

Using this technique, you can test the energy of your house, your workplace, or your bed. For example, sit down on the edge of your bed, holding the pendulum above your open palm. If it swings alongside your hand, the bed area is okay—and if it doesn't, then it is not!

You can evaluate every part of your sleeping space in the same way. After each swing of the pendulum, move up about 12 inches (30cm) until you have checked out the entire bed.

Working with Pendulum Charts

In order to make it easier to work with the pendulum, this book focuses on working with charts. Some of these charts presuppose quite a bit of expert knowledge. Take, for example, the I Ching pendulum chart. Without a basic knowledge of the structure and the inner essence of this wisdom oracle, that particular chart will be of little use to you.

Or consider the "aura soma" pendulum chart. Applying these essences calls for training or going for expert consultation and advice.

The deep knowledge of these individual techniques and practices is not described in this book. Therefore, we recommend that you find out for yourself about the individual topics in detail.

The individual pendulum charts generally speak for themselves. In each case, few individual explanations are necessary in order to understand their meaning. Use your own creativity to deal with the charts to the fullest extent.

Remember that only when the question is asked in the right way can a correct answer follow.

If you are not a therapist, use the therapeutic pendulum charts only for yourself and only as preventative or supportive measures—such as influencing the possible course of a disease in a healing way.

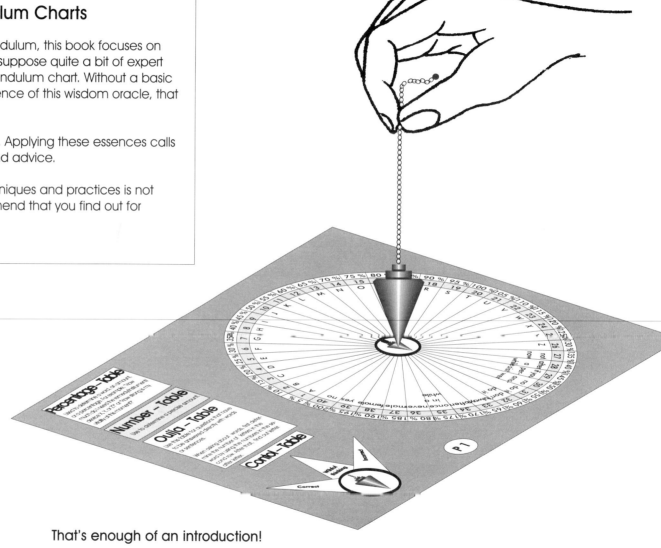

That's enough of an introduction!

Have lots of fun swinging the pendulum!

The Accuracy of Your Pendulum

Before you begin to work, test your pendulum's accuracy. If the pendulum, for example, is 75% accurate, it means that 25% of your questions are being answered incorrectly. Always pay attention to the accuracy of your pendulum when you evaluate your questions. If your pendulum capability lies below 60%, it is not worthwhile for you to swing the pendulum at this time. Use the chart to the right to ask about the reasons for this—or try again at a later time.

Remember, in any case, that the answer you get will refer to the present moment only, and can partially or completely change at another time or in another place.

Incorrect Pendulum Results

If the force of your pendulum is too weak, or if you receive an "incorrect" answer to a control question, you can determine the reasons for it with the chart below.

Pendulum Accuracy

0 % 10 % 20 % 30 % 40 % 50 % 60 % 70 % 80 % 90 % 100%

Incorrect Pendulum Results chart

- Cause unknown
- Fatigue
- Physically weak through illness
- Tension—the wrong body posture
- Lack of concentration—mental force too weak
- Influenced by cosmic rhythms
- Too egoistic a question
- Too strong wishful thinking or preconceived opinion
- Disturbances in your aura
- Wrong formulation of the question
- Wrong time to swing the pendulum (use time table below)
- Too quick interpretation (you are too excited, have too many thoughts)
- Lack of inner and/or outer calm
- Influence of other people

Control Table

Correct · Wishful Thinking · Incorrect

Always use the control chart on the right to evaluate your pendulum results.
Keep in mind:
    No answer is infallible.

The Pendulum Clock helps to determine the correct time to use the pendulum. The clock is divided into 10-minute segments.

PENDULUM

CLOCK

1 2 3 4 5 6 7 8 9 10 11 12 13 14 15 16 17 18 19 20 21 22 23 24

The Right Pendulum Chart

Which pendulum chart will give the best solution to my problem—X, Y, or Z?

or

Which pendulum chart should I work with today?

or

Which pendulum chart will give me the information I need at this moment?

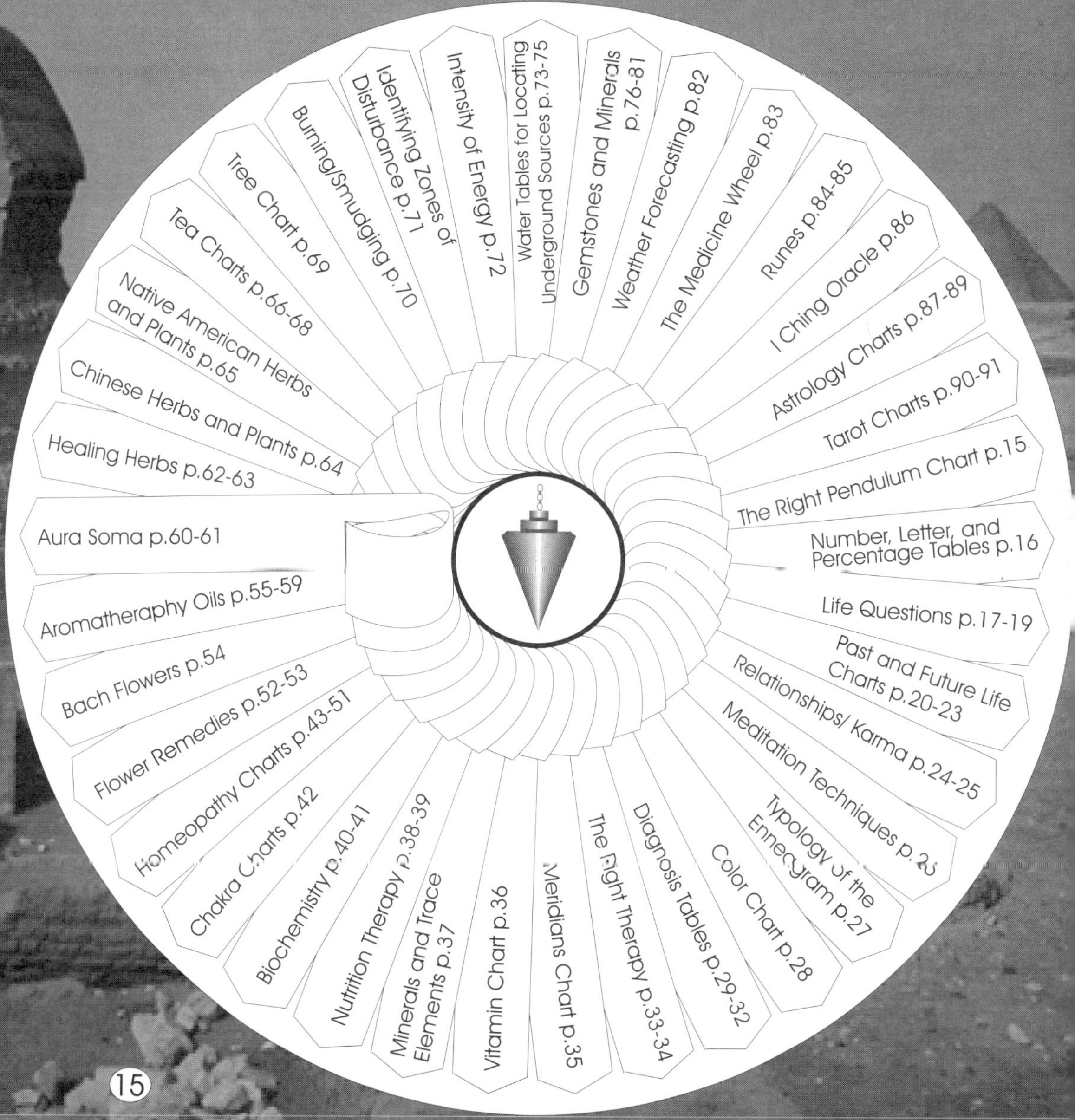

Control Table

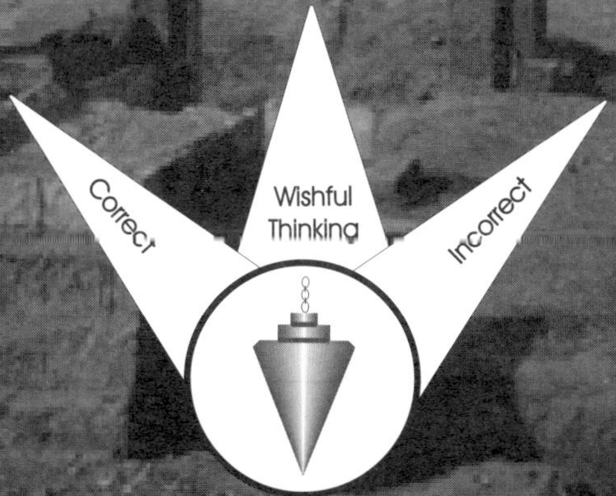

Correct

Wishful Thinking

Incorrect

NUMBER, LETTER, AND PERCENTAGE TABLES

These tables are used to determine a word, an amount, or a percentage. For example, "How much do I need the remedy/instrument/device X, Y, or Z?" or "How strong is my vitality at this moment?"

Number Table

Use this table to determine a precise amount. You can also use it to determine numbers to play in a lottery.

Ouija Table

Use this table for questions that have to be answered directly with words or sentences. When asking about words, first determine the number of letters in the word by using the numbers in the second row. After that, find out letter after letter.

Control Table

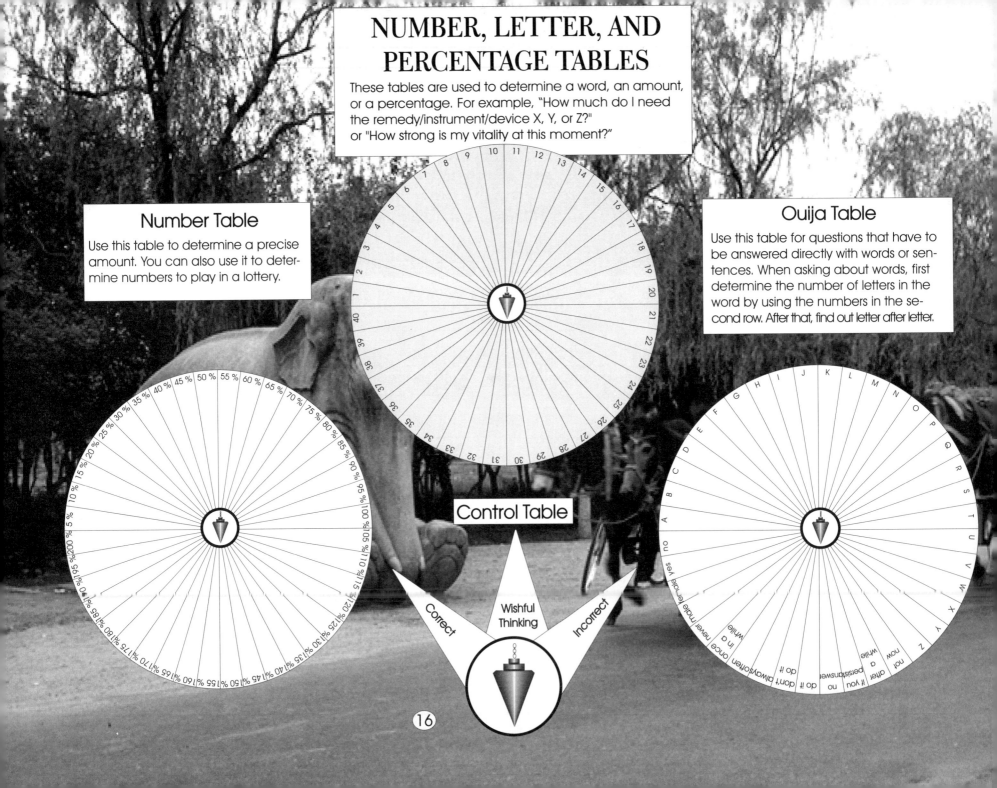

Life Questions

What obstacles are before me/X in this situation?

How will my/X's relationship with _____ develop?

- Ability to be part of a team
- Education
- Initiative
- Spiritual orientation
- Marriage /partnership
- Sexuality
- Desire for admiration
- Money/matter
- Health
- Egotism

Left Table

Right Table

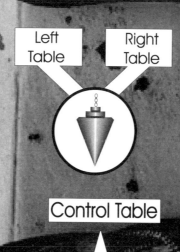

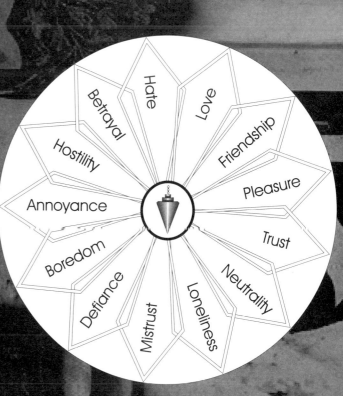

- Hate
- Love
- Betrayal
- Friendship
- Hostility
- Pleasure
- Annoyance
- Trust
- Boredom
- Neutrality
- Defiance
- Loneliness
- Mistrust

Control Table

Correct

Wishful Thinking

Incorrect

Life Questions

What virtues do I need to develop?

- Gratitude
- Honor or dignity
- Good behavior
- Adaptability
- Gentleness
- Caution
- Circumspection
- Generosity
- Conscientiousness
- Flexibility or indulgence
- Faith
- Courage
- Discretion
- Dignity
- Devotion

- Understanding
- Unselfishness
- Humility
- Sympathy
- Kindness
- Smarts
- Loyalty
- Sincerity
- Mercy or compassion
- Simplicity
- Respect
- Reason/good sense
- Perseverance
- Patience
- Modesty

What vices do I need to get rid of?

- Intrigue
- Arrogance
- Avarice
- Intolerance
- Boasting
- Ingratitude
- Brutality
- Indecency
- Carelessness or recklessness
- Hypocrisy
- Cowardice
- Faithlessness or infidelity
- Cruelty
- Envy
- Egotism

- Viciousness
- Jealousy
- Malice or spite
- Vanity
- Malicious joy in others' misfortunes
- Untruth
- Mistrust
- Thirst for revenge
- Pettiness
- Thirst for pleasure
- Pride
- Talking too much
- Showing off
- Superficiality
- Stubbornness

Control Table

- Table left top
- Table right top
- Table left below
- Table right below

- Correct
- Wishful Thinking
- Incorrect

18

Life Questions

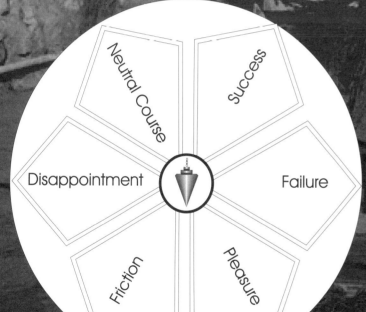

Destiny Question
How does the event_____ end?

Neutral Course

Success

Disappointment

Failure

Friction

Pleasure

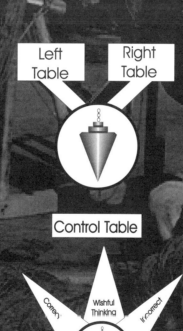

Left Table

Right Table

Control Table

Correct

Wishful Thinking

Incorrect

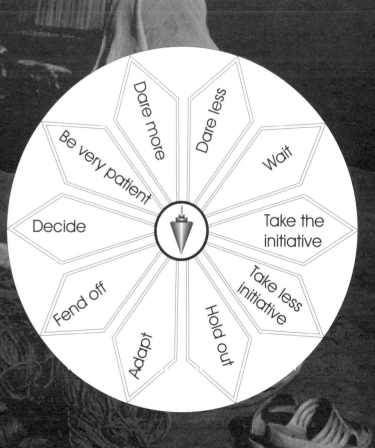

Destiny Question
What shall I do in case_____?

Dare more

Dare less

Be very patient

Wait

Decide

Take the initiative

Fend off

Take less initiative

Adapt

Hold out

Past and Future Life Charts

Find out, by swinging the pendulum, and with the help of the charts below, which incarnation in the past or future is most important for you.

Find out, by swinging the pendulum, the exact date of the incarnation (begin below). Determine ahead of time whether you want to find out the birthday or the day of death.

Incarnations in the Past

4. Back
3. Back
2. Back
5. Back
1. Back
6. Back
This Life
7. Back
12. Back
8. Back
11. Back
9. Back
10. Back

Left Table
Right Table

Information in the Future

3. Forward
2. Forward
4. Forward
1. Forward
5. Forward
This Life
6. Forward
7. Forward
12. Forward
8. Forward
11. Forward
9. Forward
10. Forward

Control Table

Correct
Wishful Thinking
Incorrect

Day

1. 2. 3. 4. 5. 6. 7. 8. 9. 10. 11. 12. 13. 14. 15. 16. 17. 18. 19. 20. 21. 22. 23. 24. 25. 26. 27. 28. 29. 30. 31.

Month

January, February, March, April, May, June, July, August, September, October, November, December

Year

0, 1, 2, 3, 4, 5, 6, 7, 8, 9

Decade

0-10, 10-20, 20-30, 30-40, 40-50, 50-60, 60-70, 70-80, 80-90, 90-100

Century

0-100, 100-200, 200-300, 300-400, 400-500, 500-600, 600-700, 700-800, 800-900, 900-1000

Millennium

9000-10000 BC, 8000-9000 BC, 7000-8000 BC, 6000-7000 BC, 5000-6000 BC, 4000-5000 BC, 3000-4000 BC, 2000-3000 BC, 1000-2000 BC, 0-1000 BC, 0-1000 AD, 1000-2000 AD, 2000-3000 AD, 3000-4000 AD, 4000-5000 AD, 5000-6000 AD, 6000-7000 AD, 7000-8000 AD, 8000-9000 AD, 9000-10000 AD

Geographical Orientation of the Incarnation

North America

Europe

Asia

Africa

South America

Atlantis

Lemuria

Australia

Another Planet

Control Table

Correct

Wishful Thinking

Incorrect

If you find your continent and need more detailed information, find an atlas and ask for the precise location on your continent.

Life Circumstances of the Incarnation

In order to find out the name of your previous important incarnation as well as the years it took place, use the pendulum chart on page 16.

Change of gender in previous incarnation and probable cause

Sex in this Incarnation

Male   Female

Control Table

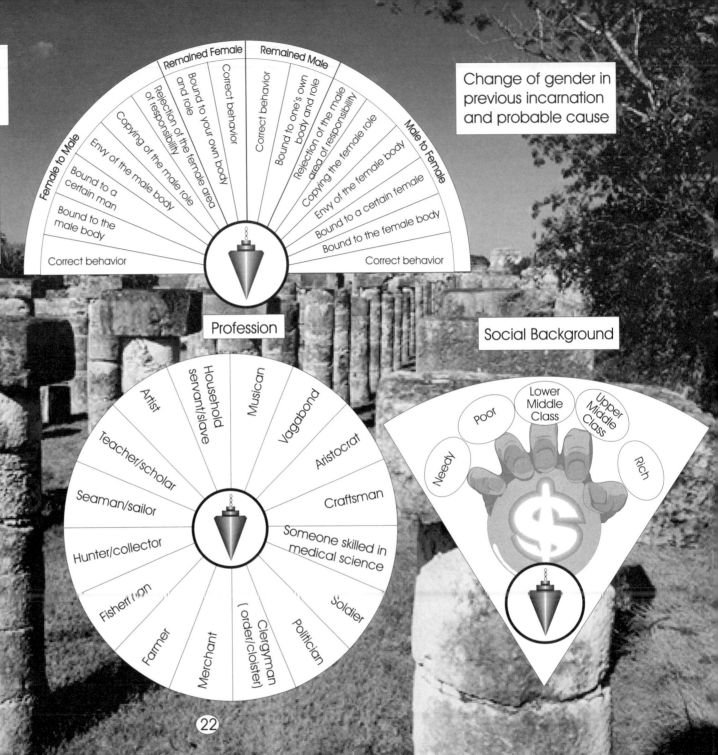

Change of gender chart (Profession pendulum)

Female to Male:
- Correct behavior
- Bound to the male body
- Bound to a certain man
- Envy of the male body
- Copying of the male role
- Rejection of the female area of responsibility
- Bound to your own body and role

Remained Female:
- Correct behavior

Remained Male:
- Correct behavior
- Bound to one's own body and role
- Rejection of the male area of responsibility
- Copying the female role
- Envy of the female body
- Bound to a certain female
- Bound to the female body

Male to Female:
- Correct behavior

Profession

- Household servant/slave
- Musican
- Vagabond
- Aristocrat
- Craftsman
- Someone skilled in medical science
- Soldier
- Politician
- Clergyman (order/cloister)
- Merchant
- Farmer
- Fisherman
- Hunter/collector
- Seaman/sailor
- Teacher/scholar
- Artist

Social Background

- Needy
- Poor
- Lower Middle Class
- Upper Middle Class
- Rich

Control Table:
- Correct
- Wishful Thinking
- Incorrect

22

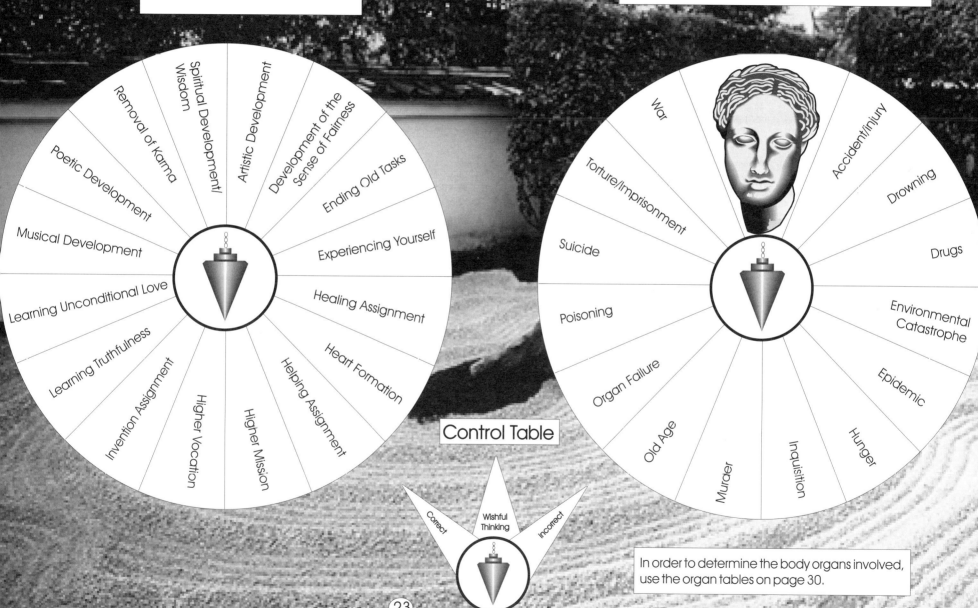

Life Work of the Incarnation

- Spiritual Development/Wisdom
- Artistic Development
- Development of the Sense of Fairness
- Ending Old Tasks
- Experiencing Yourself
- Healing Assignment
- Heart Formation
- Helping Assignment
- Higher Mission
- Higher Vocation
- Invention Assignment
- Learning Truthfulness
- Learning Unconditional Love
- Musical Development
- Poetic Development
- Removal of Karma

Death of the Incarnation

- War
- Accident/injury
- Torture/Imprisonment
- Drowning
- Suicide
- Drugs
- Poisoning
- Environmental Catastrophe
- Organ Failure
- Epidemic
- Old Age
- Hunger
- Murder
- Inquisition

Control Table

Correct · Wishful Thinking · Incorrect

In order to determine the body organs involved, use the organ tables on page 30.

Karmic Relationships

To find out if a relationship is karmic, use the table. If yes, ask whether the relationship will last over the course of several incarnations.

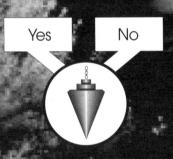

Yes   No

Control Table

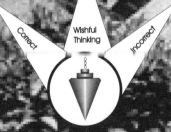

Correct   Wishful Thinking   Incorrect

Someone Whom You Met Once · Spouse · Lover · Mother · Father · Daughter · Son · Sister · Brother · Uncle · Aunt · Niece · Nephew · Female Cousin · Male Cousin · Distantly Related · Friend (Female) · Friend (Male) · Female Acquaintance · Male Acquaintance

What feelings existed in the karmic relationship?

Respect · Friendship · Reverence · Emotional Dependence · Contempt · Resentment · Hostility · Hate · Deep Love · Infatuation

What relationship existed in the last incarnation? Find out by swinging the pendulum in the first reincarnation chart, which will tell you which life and when you met the person.

Higher Karmic Laws

The Four Phases of Karma

Why am I the way I am? Why does this or that happen to me? Why do I have to live under these circumstances? According to Indian philosophy, all karmic reactions manifest in four different phases:

1 Phase (Bija = the seed)—Actions and intentions exist only as wishes—in the fine material area.
"Sow a thought and you will harvest a deed."

2 Phase (Kuta-stha = the conscious resolution)—The wish becomes deed. Karmic chain reactions can be triggered.
"Sow a deed and you will harvest a habit."

3 Phase (Phalonmukha = the bearing of fruits)—The material actions bear fruit.
"Sow a habit and you will harvest a character."

4 Phase (Prarabdha = harvest)—The karmic reaction has occurred in the present life.
"Sow a character and you will harvest a destiny."

The Art of Karma

Karma
Acting according to the laws of nature
=Material happiness

Vikarma
Acting against the laws of nature
=Sorrow

Akarma
Transcendental acting outside the laws of karma
=Liberation

Collective karma
Acting with the masses
=Sorrow

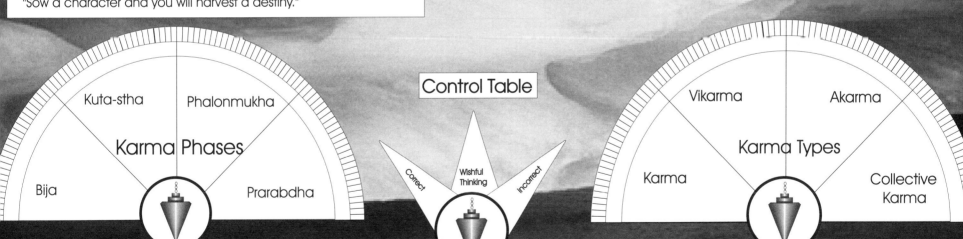

Karma Phases — Kuta-stha, Phalonmukha, Bija, Prarabdha

Control Table — Correct, Wishful Thinking, Incorrect

Karma Types — Vikarma, Akarma, Karma, Collective Karma

Meditation Techniques

Which type of meditation is best for me (or X) at the moment?

- Mantra Meditation
- Mandala Meditation
- Listening and keeping silent
- Light/Color Meditation
- Kundalini Meditation
- Gemstone Meditation
- Dynamic Meditation
- Chakra Meditation
- Breathing Meditation
- Autogenous Training
- Meditation to Music
- Nature Experience
- Prayer
- Tai Chi Chuan
- Transcendental Meditation
- Visual Meditation
- Walking Meditation
- Yoga
- Zen Meditation

Control Table

- Correct
- Wishful Thinking
- Incorrect

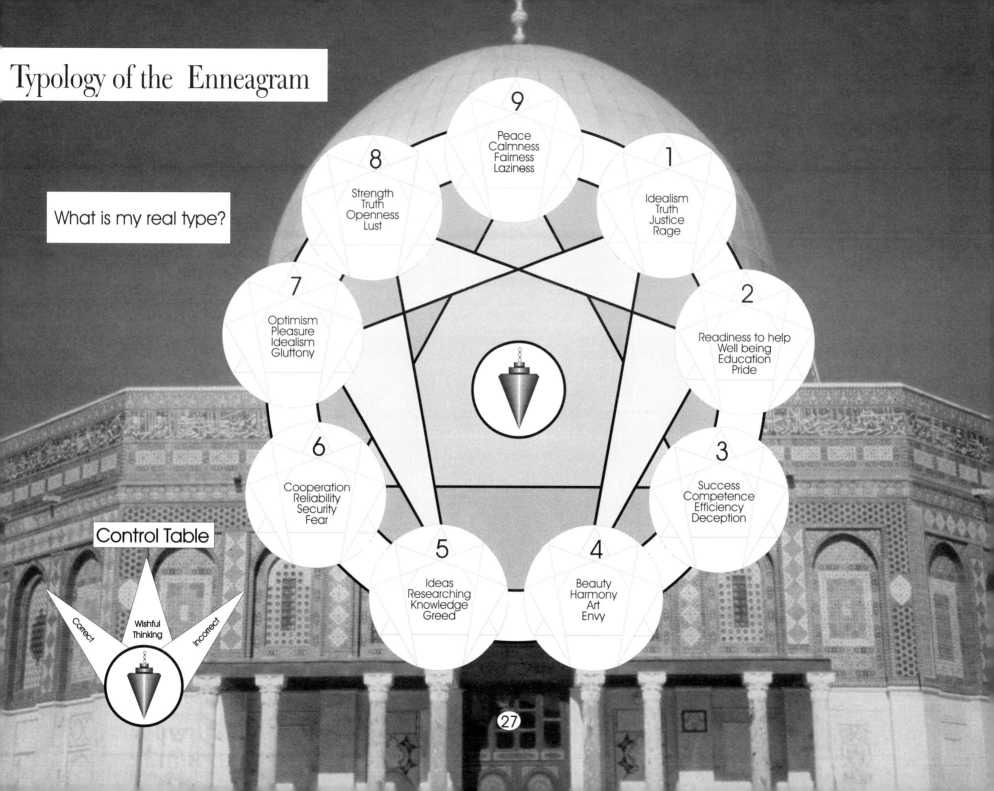

Typology of the Enneagram

What is my real type?

9
Peace
Calmness
Fairness
Laziness

8
Strength
Truth
Openness
Lust

1
Idealism
Truth
Justice
Rage

7
Optimism
Pleasure
Idealism
Gluttony

2
Readiness to help
Well being
Education
Pride

6
Cooperation
Reliability
Security
Fear

3
Success
Competence
Efficiency
Deception

5
Ideas
Researching
Knowledge
Greed

4
Beauty
Harmony
Art
Envy

Control Table

Correct
Wishful Thinking
Incorrect

Color Chart

What colors do I (or X) need to work with?
Ask if several colors are needed.

How shall I work with the color?

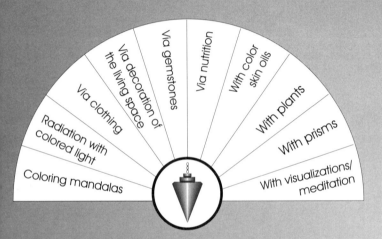

- Via gemstones
- Via decoration of the living space
- Via clothing
- Via nutrition
- With color skin oils
- Radiation with colored light
- With plants
- Coloring mandalas
- With prisms
- With visualizations/meditation

Control Table

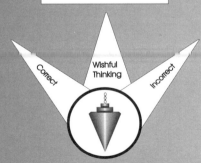

- Correct
- Wishful Thinking
- Incorrect

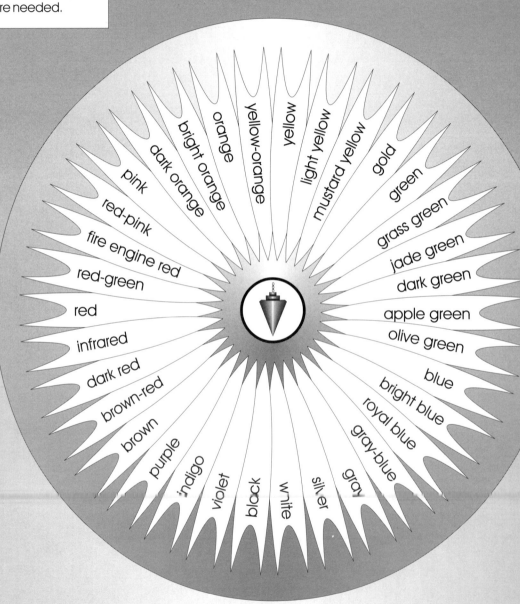

- pink
- dark orange
- bright orange
- orange
- yellow-orange
- yellow
- light yellow
- mustard yellow
- gold
- red-pink
- green
- fire engine red
- grass green
- red-green
- jade green
- red
- dark green
- infrared
- apple green
- dark red
- olive green
- brown-red
- blue
- brown
- bright blue
- purple
- royal blue
- indigo
- gray-blue
- violet
- gray
- black
- white
- silver

Diagnosis Tables

Physical causes of the illness

What has caused this illness?

Psychic causes of the illness

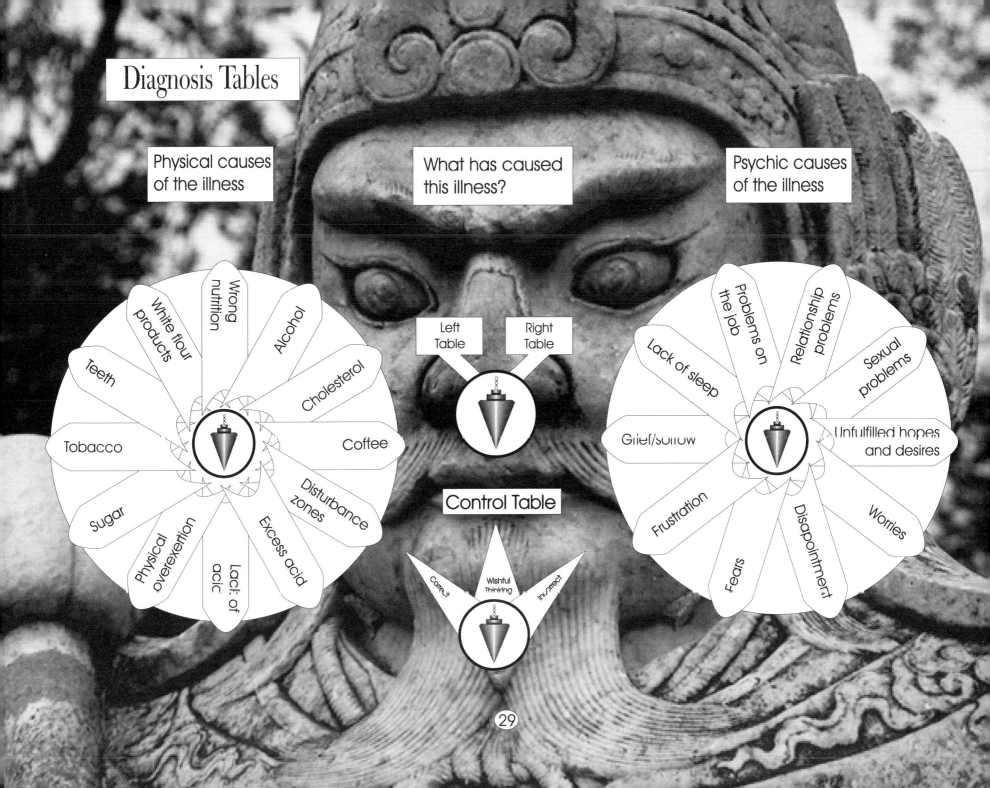

Physical causes table:
- Wrong nutrition
- Alcohol
- Cholesterol
- Coffee
- Disturbance zones
- Excess acid
- Lack of acid
- Physical overexertion
- Sugar
- Tobacco
- Teeth
- White flour products

Left Table / Right Table

Psychic causes table:
- Problems on the job
- Relationship problems
- Sexual problems
- Unfulfilled hopes and desires
- Worries
- Disappointment
- Fears
- Frustration
- Grief/sorrow
- Lack of sleep

Control Table

Correct / Wishful Thinking / Incorrect

Diagnosis Tables

Area of health disturbance

What areas are afflicted by the illness?
At which areas should treatment begin?

Areas of the inner organs

Vital Power

Acids, excess of

Skeleton

Acids, lack of

Reproductive system

Blood circulation system

Nervous system

Breathing

Lymphatic system

Digestion

Heart

Glands

Left table

Right table

Control Table

Correct

Wishful Thinking

Incorrect

Thymus gland

Uretha

Uterus

Veins

Appendix

Testicles/ovaries

Arteries

Suprarenal glands

Bile

Spleen

Bladder

Spinal cord

Bronchia/lungs

Small intestine

Duodenum

Esophagus /stomach

Skin

Gall bladder

Rectum/gut

Heart

Pancreas

Muscles/sinews

Lymph paths

Liver

Larnyx

Kidneys

Diagnosis Tables

Head—Neck

Skeleton

What areas are afflicted by the illness?
or
At which areas should treatment begin?

Left Table

Right Table

Head—Neck wheel
- Thyroid
- Tonsils
- Cerebellum
- Cerebrum
- Throat
- Ears
- Teeth
- Eyes
- Sinus
- Hair
- Pituitary
- Head/neck
- Pineal gland
- Meninges
- Nose?
- Mouth

Skeleton wheel
- Shoulder/collarbone
- Skull
- Spine/disks
- Ankle
- Shinbone
- Arms
- Upper thighs
- Chest/ribs
- Pelvis/buttocks
- Elbow/joint
- Nails/feet
- Feet/toes
- Nails/hands
- Hands/fingers
- Knee
- Hands/knuckles
- Jaw
- Hip joint

Control Table

- Correct
- Wishful Thinking
- Incorrect

31

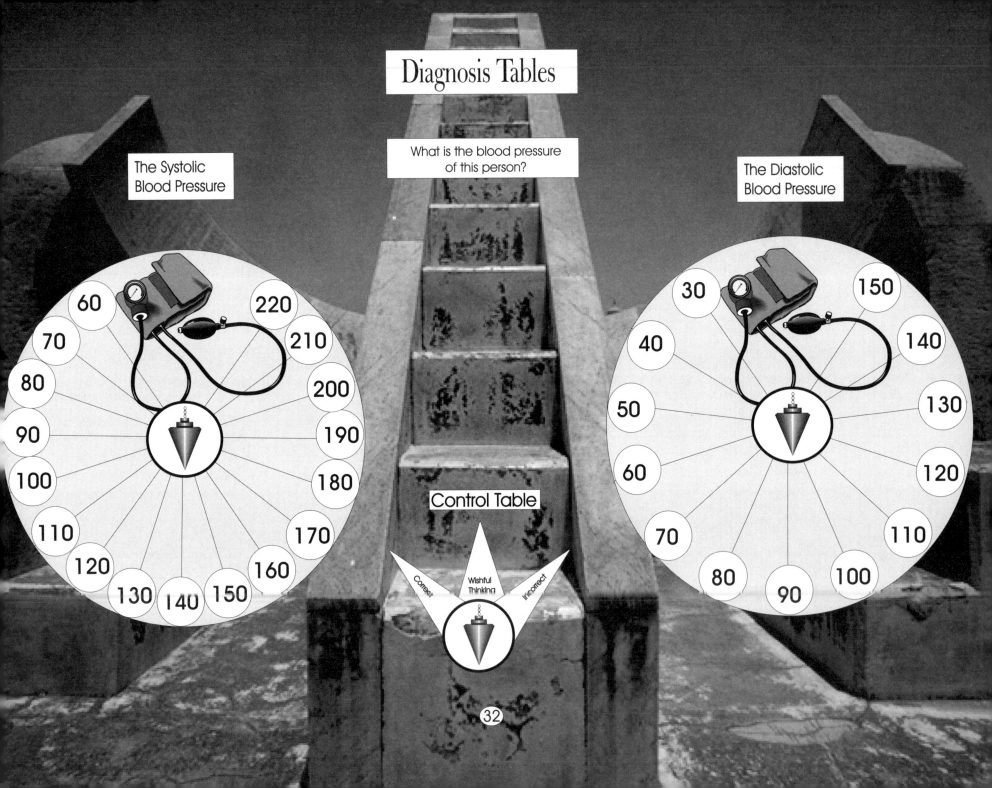

Diagnosis Tables

What is the blood pressure of this person?

The Systolic Blood Pressure

The Diastolic Blood Pressure

Control Table

Correct   Wishful Thinking   Incorrect

32

Also, several therapies may be necessary. Using the number chart on page 16, ask how many will be needed, and then swing the pendulum to find them individually.

Control Table

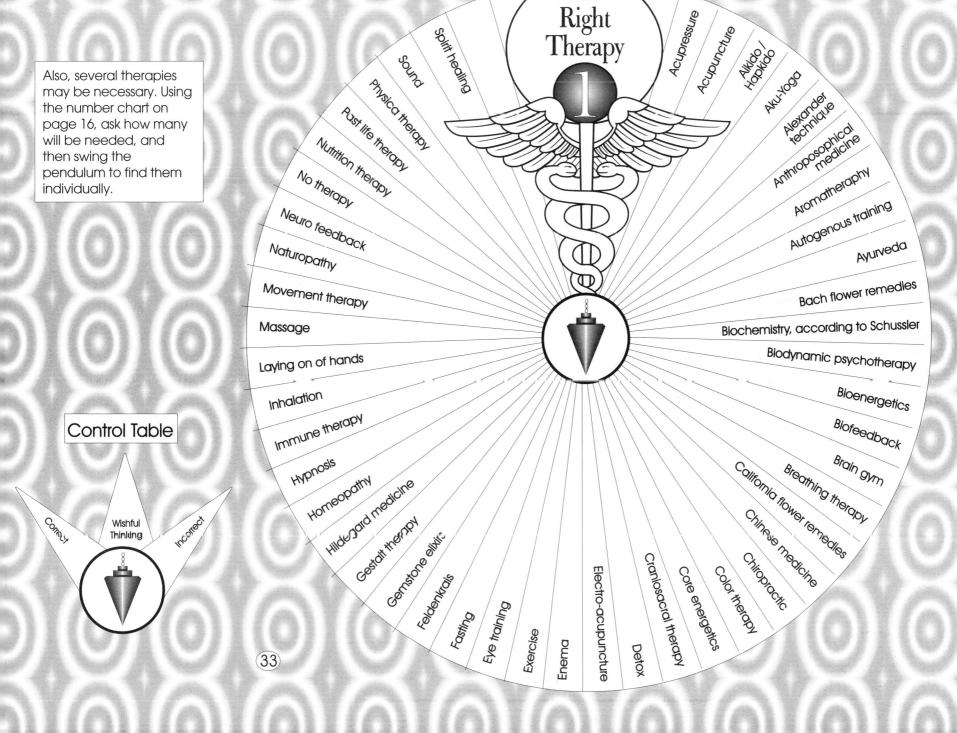

The Right Therapy
1

Acupressure
Acupuncture
Aikido / Hapkido
Aku-Yoga
Alexander technique
Anthroposophical medicine
Aromatheraphy
Autogenous training
Ayurveda
Bach flower remedies
Biochemistry, according to Schussler
Biodynamic psychotherapy
Bioenergetics
Biofeedback
Brain gym
Breathing therapy
California flower remedies
Chinese medicine
Chiropractic
Color therapy
Core energetics
Craniosacral therapy
Detox
Electro-acupuncture
Enema
Exercise
Eye training
Fasting
Feldenkrais
Gemstone elixir
Gestalt therapy
Hildegard medicine
Homeopathy
Hypnosis
Immune therapy
Inhalation
Laying on of hands
Massage
Movement therapy
Naturopathy
Neuro feedback
No therapy
Nutrition therapy
Past life therapy
Physica therapy
Sound
Spirit healing

Correct · Wishful Thinking · Incorrect

33

Several other therapies may be necessary. Using the number chart on page 16, find out how many are needed, and then swing the pendulum to find them.

Control Table

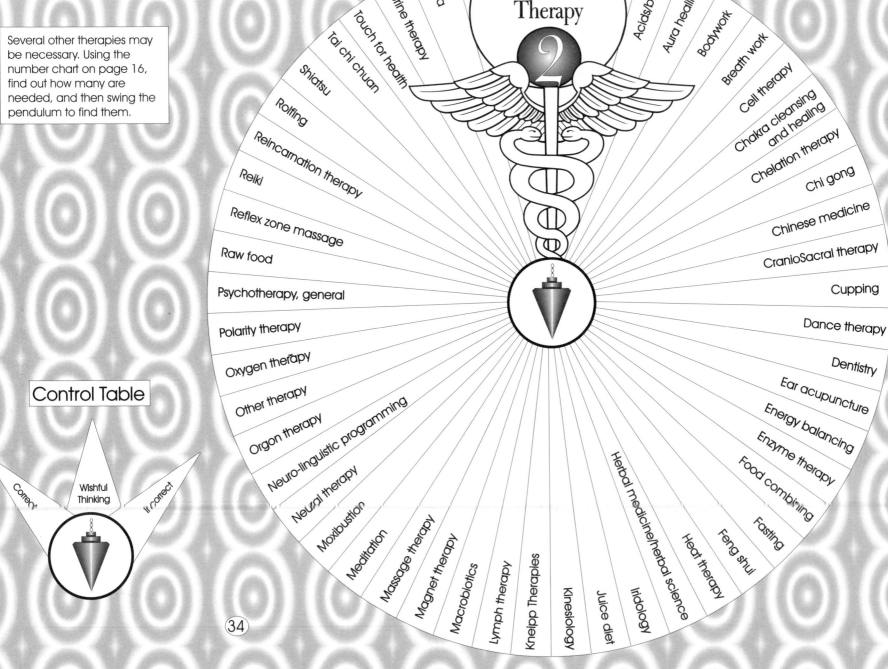

The Right Therapy

2

Yoga
Urine therapy
Touch for health
Tai chi chuan
Shiatsu
Rolfing
Reincarnation therapy
Reiki
Reflex zone massage
Raw food
Psychotherapy, general
Polarity therapy
Oxygen therapy
Other therapy
Orgon therapy
Neuro-linguistic programming
Neural therapy
Moxibustion
Meditation
Massage therapy
Magnet therapy
Macrobiotics
Lymph therapy
Kneipp Therapies
Kinesiology
Juice diet
Iridology
Herbal medicine/herbal science
Heat therapy
Feng shui
Fasting
Food combining
Enzyme therapy
Energy balancing
Ear acupuncture
Dentistry
Dance therapy
Cupping
CranioSacral therapy
Chinese medicine
Chi gong
Chelation therapy
Chakra cleansing and healing
Cell therapy
Breath work
Bodywork
Aura healing
Acids/bases

Correct
Wishful Thinking
Incorrect

(34)

Meridian Chart

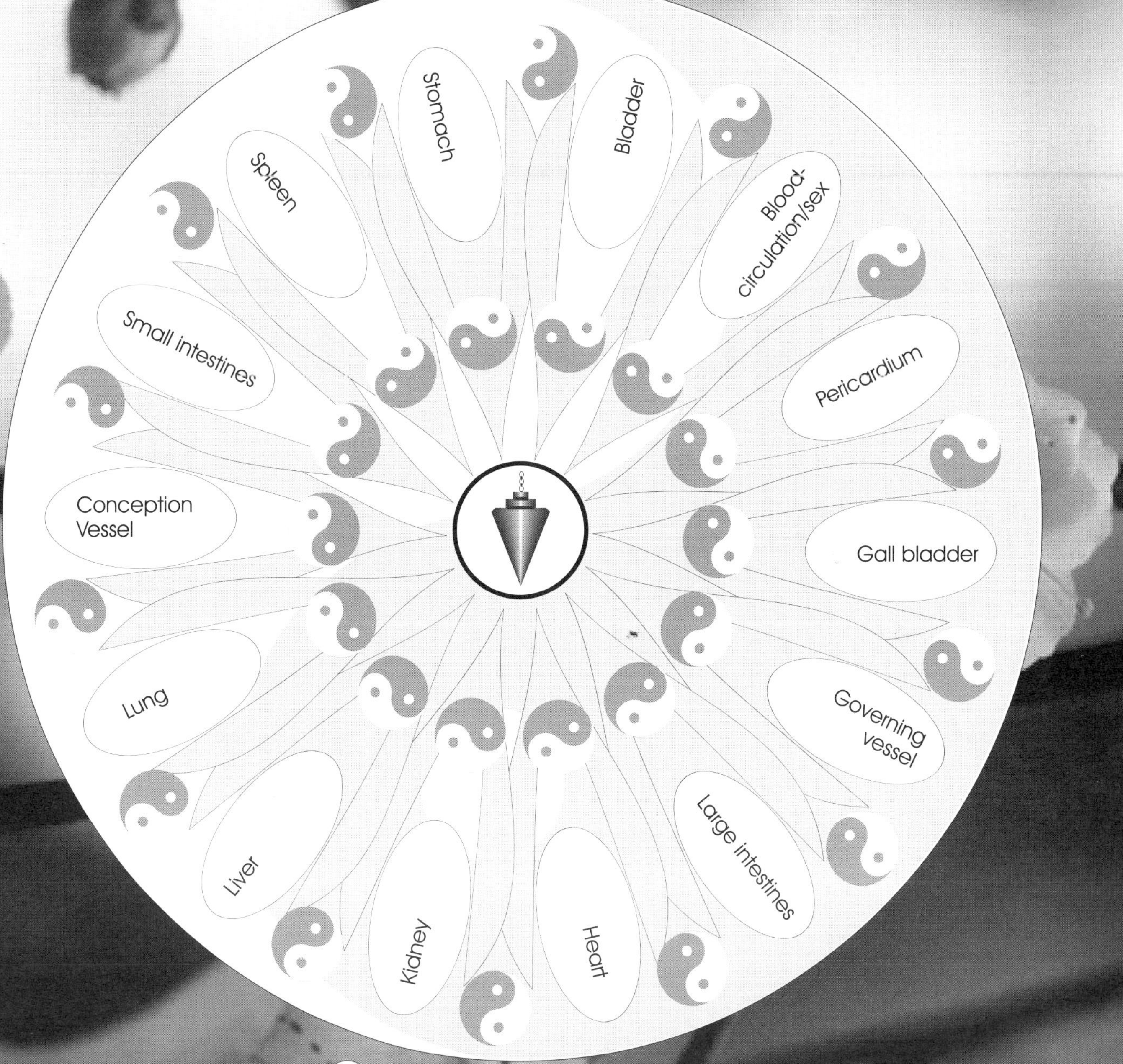
Stomach
Bladder
Blood-circulation/sex
Pericardium
Gall bladder
Governing vessel
Large intestines
Heart
Kidney
Liver
Lung
Conception Vessel
Small intestines
Spleen

Control Table

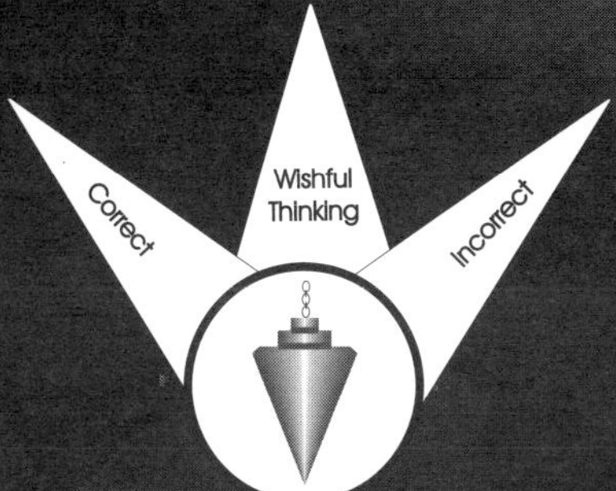
Correct
Wishful Thinking
Incorrect

Vitamin Table

U A B 1 B 2 B 3 B 6 B 12 B complex Biotin C Coenzyme Q-10 D E Echinacea Evening Primrose oil Folic acid Garlic Ginseng Gotu Kola Green Tea Inositol K Kelp Melatonin Niacin

Control Table

Correct Wishful Thinking Incorrect

36

Minerals and
Trace Elements

- Water
- Zinc
- Calcium
- Chlorine
- Chromium
- Cobalt
- Copper
- Fluoride
- Iodine
- Iron
- Magnesium
- Manganese
- Molybdenum
- Niacin
- Phosphorus
- Potassium
- Selenium
- Sodium
- Sulphur
- Vanadium

Control Table

- Correct
- Wishful Thinking
- Incorrect

Nutrition Therapy— Shoots and Sprouts

Which chart should be used?
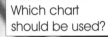

Shoots/Sprouts · Grass Juices

How many kinds of sprouts should be eaten?

1 2 3 4 5 6 7 8 9 10 11 12 13 14 15 16 17 18 19 20

How often should the shoots/sprouts be eaten?

3 x daily · 4 x daily · 2 x daily · 5 x daily · 1 x daily · 6 x daily · 10 x daily · 7 x daily · 9 x daily · 8 x daily

What amounts should be eaten?
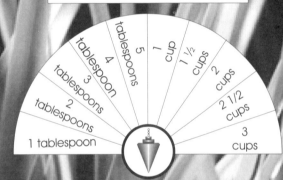

5 tablespoons · 4 tablespoons · 3 tablespoons · 2 tablespoons · 1 tablespoon · 1 cup · 1 ½ cups · 2 cups · 2 1/2 cups · 3 cups

Control Table

Correct · Wishful Thinking · Incorrect

How much grass juice should be taken?

3 6 10 13 17 20 24 27 31 34 68
Fluid ounces grass juice

How long should the shoots/sprouts be eaten?

3 Months · 4 Months · 2 Months · 3 Weeks · 4 Weeks · 5 Months · 3 Days · 4 Days · 5 Weeks · 2 Weeks · 2 Days · 5 Days · 6 Months · 1 Month · 1 Week · 1 Day · 6 Days · 6 Weeks · 7 Months · 7 Days · 10 Weeks · 8 Days · 8 Months · 9 Weeks · 8 Weeks · 9 Days · 10 Months · 9 Months

Nutrition Therapy

Shoots and Sprouts

Adzuki beans
Alfalfa
Barley
Buckwheat
Chick peas
Cress
Fenugreek
Lentils
Linseed
Millet
Mung beans
Mustard
Peas
Pumpkins
Radishes
Rye
Sesame
Soybeans, yellow
Sunflower seeds
Wheat

Grass Juices

Wheat grass
Barley grass
Oat grass
Rye grass

Control Table

Correct
Wishful Thinking
Incorrect

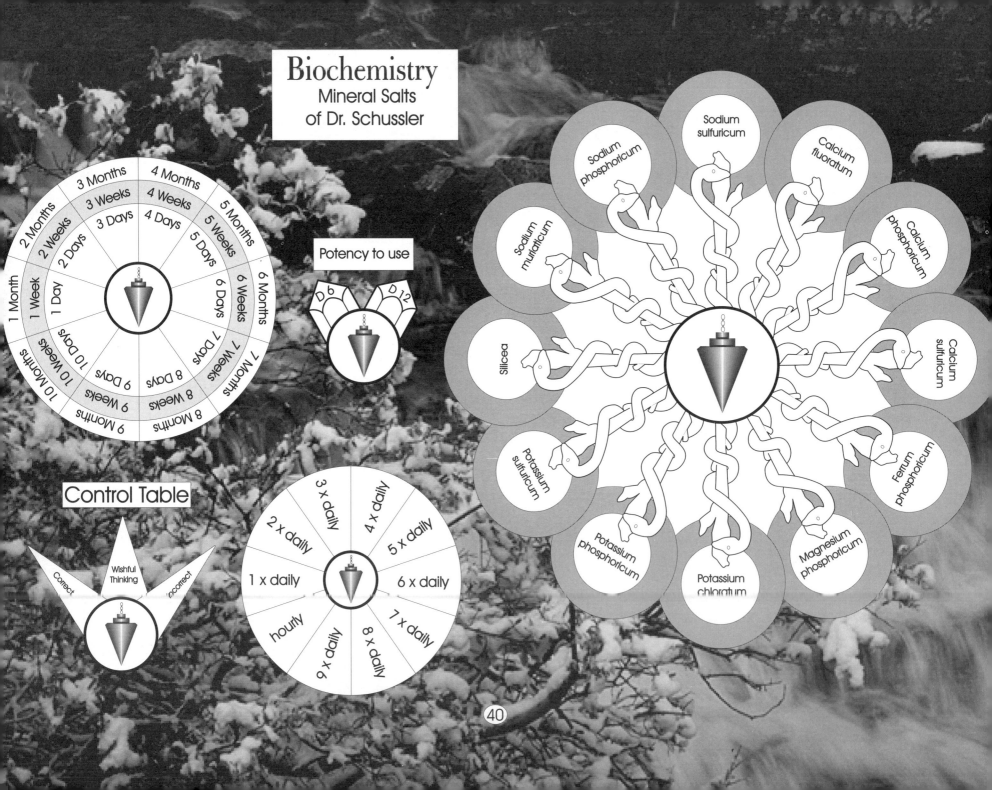

Biochemistry
Mineral Salts of Dr. Schussler

Potency to use

D 6   D 12

Control Table

Correct   Wishful Thinking   Incorrect

3 x daily
4 x daily
2 x daily
5 x daily
1 x daily
6 x daily
hourly
7 x daily
9 x daily
8 x daily

Sodium phosphoricum
Sodium sulfuricum
Calcium fluoratum
Sodium muriaticum
Calcium phosphoricum
Silicea
Calcium sulfuricum
Potassium sulfuricum
Ferrum phosphoricum
Potassium phosphoricum
Potassium chloratum
Magnesium phosphoricum

3 Months
4 Months
2 Months
3 Weeks
4 Weeks
5 Months
3 Days
4 Days
5 Weeks
1 Month
2 Weeks
2 Days
5 Days
6 Days
1 Week
1 Day
6 Weeks
6 Months
10 Months
10 Weeks
10 Days
9 Days
8 Days
7 Days
7 Weeks
7 Months
9 Months
8 Months
9 Weeks
8 Weeks

40

Biochemistry
Mineral Salts
of Dr. Schussler

3 Months · 4 Months · 3 Weeks · 4 Weeks · 5 Months · 3 Days · 4 Days · 5 Weeks · 2 Months · 5 Days · 2 Weeks · 6 Months · 2 Days · 6 Days · 1 Month · 6 Weeks · 1 Week · 1 Day · 7 Days · 7 Weeks · 10 Weeks · 7 Months · 10 Days · 8 Days · 9 Days · 8 Weeks · 10 Months · 9 Months · 8 Months · 9 Weeks

Potency to use

D 6 · D 12

Control Table

Correct · Wishful Thinking · Incorrect

3 x daily · 4 x daily · 2 x daily · 5 x daily · 1 x daily · 6 x daily · hourly · 7 x daily · 9 x daily · 8 x daily

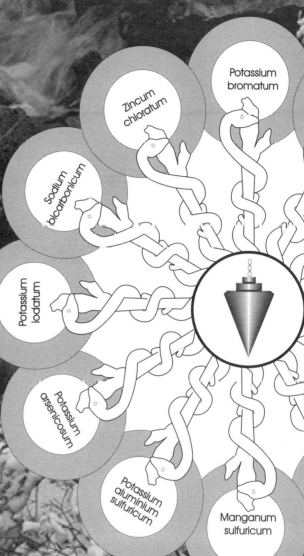

Zincum chloratum · Potassium bromatum · Arsenum iodatum · Sodium bicarbonicum · Calcium sulfuricum · Potassium iodatum · Calcium carbonicum · Potassium arsenicosum · Cuprum arsenicosum · Potassium aluminium sulfuricum · Manganum sulfuricum · Lithium chloratum

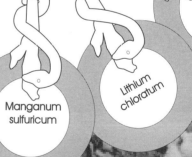

Chakra Table

Under-energized Balanced Over-energized

Under-energized — Balanced — Over-energized

-100 % ... -5 %, 0 %, 5 % ... 100 %

Control Table

Correct

Wishful Thinking

Incorrect

7. Chakra
Skull, cerebrum, pineal gland

violet, white, gold

1. Chakra
Spine, bones, legs, rectum, intestines, blood, suprarenal gland

red

6. Chakra
Nose, ears, eyes, face, cerebellum, pituitary gland

indigo blue, violet

5. Chakra
Voice, throat, bronchia, top part of lung, thyroid

light blue

2. Chakra
Reproductive system, digestion, kidneys, prostate, gonad, ovaries, testicles

orange

3. Chakra
Liver, stomach, bile, nervous system, pancreas

yellow/ golden yellow

4. Chakra
Heart, lower part of lung, skin, hands, thymus gland

green, pink, gold

42

Homeopathy Tables

Working with homeopathic medicines should be done by an experienced practitioner. Diagnosis and prescription require a basic knowledge of homeopathy, a lot of practice and experience with the pendulum, common sense, and practice in the medical healing science.

In what form should the medication be taken?

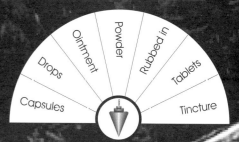

- Powder
- Ointment
- Rubbed in
- Drops
- Tablets
- Capsules
- Tincture

On which table will I find the best remedies for the person?

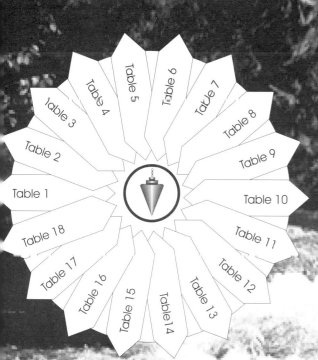

- Table 1
- Table 2
- Table 3
- Table 4
- Table 5
- Table 6
- Table 7
- Table 8
- Table 9
- Table 10
- Table 11
- Table 12
- Table 13
- Table 14
- Table 15
- Table 16
- Table 17
- Table 18

At which potency should the medication be taken?

- D - Potencies
- C Potencies
- LM - Potencies

How long should the medication be taken?

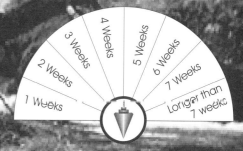

- 1 Weeks
- 2 Weeks
- 3 Weeks
- 4 Weeks
- 5 Weeks
- 6 Weeks
- 7 Weeks
- Longer than 7 weeks

Control Table

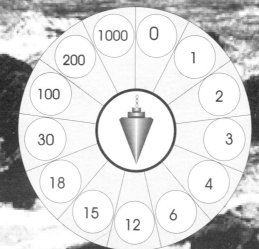

- Correct
- Wishful Thinking
- Incorrect

(43)

- 1000
- 0
- 200
- 1
- 100
- 2
- 30
- 3
- 18
- 4
- 15
- 6
- 12

How often should the medication be taken?

- Twice daily
- 3 times daily
- Once a day
- 5 times daily
- Once a week
- Hourly
- Twice a week
- One time
- 3 times a week
- Once a month

Homeopathy Tables

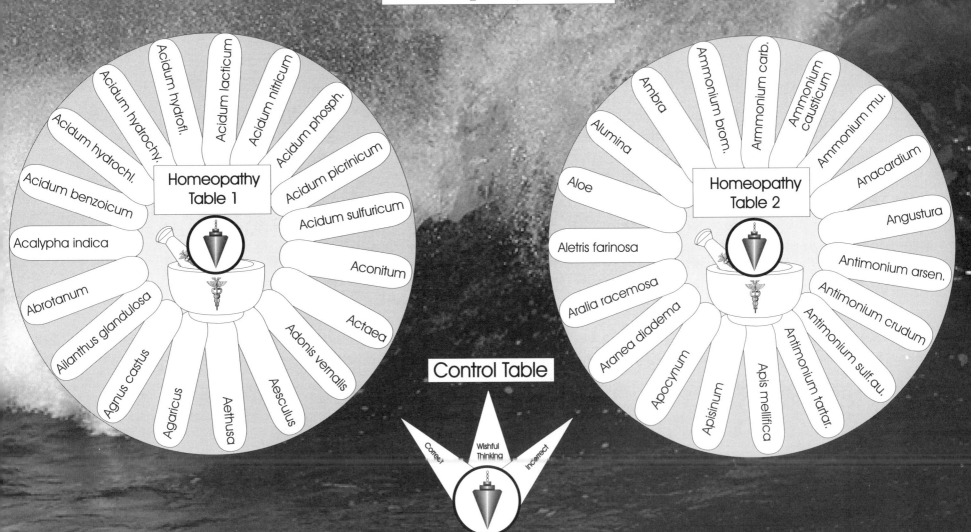

Homeopathy Table 1

Acidum hydrofl.
Acidum lacticum
Acidum nitricum
Acidum phosph.
Acidum picrinicum
Acidum sulfuricum
Aconitum
Actaea
Adonis vernalis
Aesculus
Aethusa
Agaricus
Agnus castus
Ailanthus glandulosa
Abrotanum
Acalypha indica
Acidum benzoicum
Acidum hydrochl.
Acidum hydrochy.

Homeopathy Table 2

Ammonium carb.
Ammonium causticum
Ammonium mu.
Anacardium
Angustura
Antimonium arsen.
Antimonium crudum
Antimonium sulf. au.
Antimonium tartar.
Apis mellifica
Apisinum
Apocynum
Aranea diadema
Aralia racemosa
Aletris farinosa
Aloe
Alumina
Ambra
Ammonium brom.

Control Table

Correct
Wishful Thinking
Incorrect

44

Homeopathy Tables

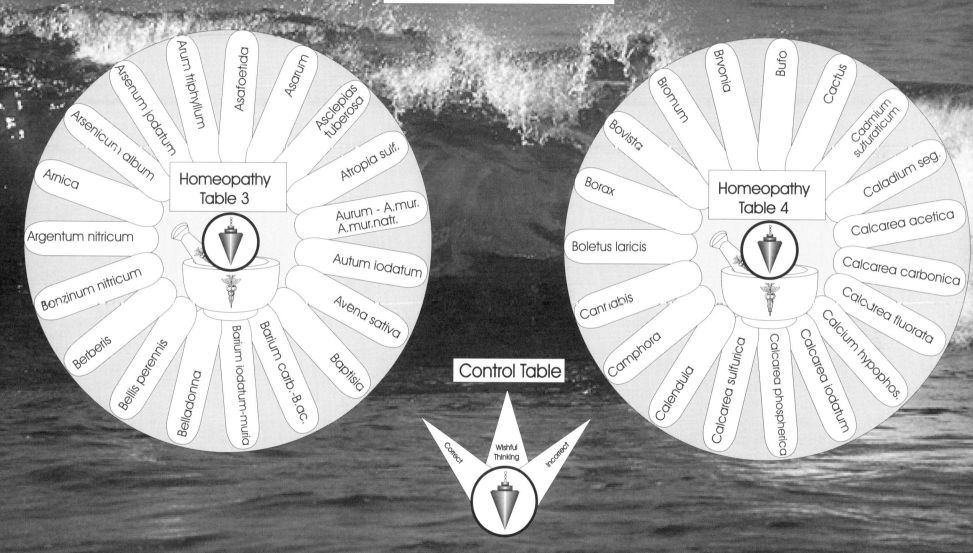

Homeopathy Table 3

- Arum triphyllum
- Asafoetida
- Asarum
- Asclepias tuberosa
- Atropia sulf.
- Aurum - A.mur, A.mur.natr.
- Autum iodatum
- Avena sativa
- Baptisia
- Barium carb.-B.ac.
- Barium iodatum-muria
- Belladonna
- Bellis perennis
- Berberis
- Bonzinum nitricum
- Argentum nitricum
- Arnica
- Arsenicum album
- Arsenum iodatum

Homeopathy Table 4

- Bryonia
- Bufo
- Cactus
- Cadmium sulfuraticum
- Caladium seg.
- Calcarea acetica
- Calcarea carbonica
- Calcarea fluorata
- Calcium hypophos.
- Calcarea iodatum
- Calcarea phospherica
- Calcarea sulfurica
- Calendula
- Camphora
- Cannabis
- Boletus laricis
- Borax
- Bovista
- Bromum

Control Table

- Correct
- Wishful Thinking
- Incorrect

Homeopathy Tables

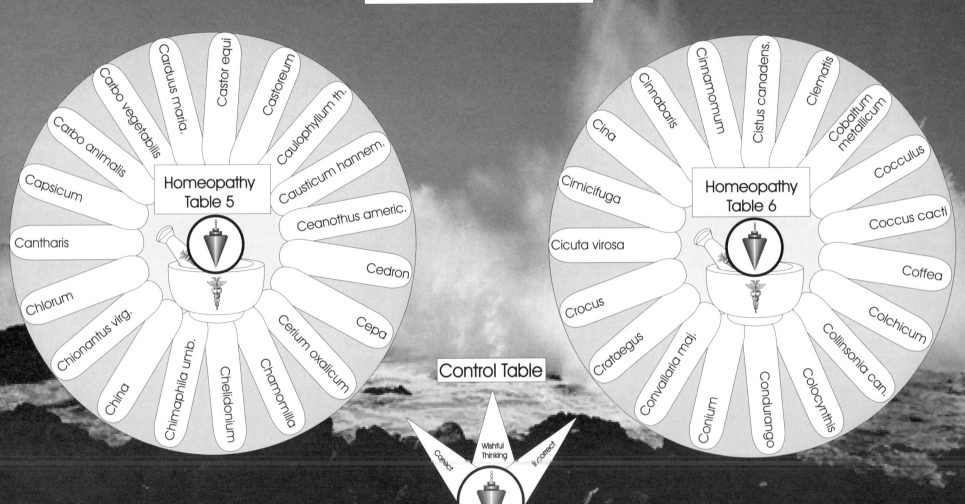

Homeopathy
Table 5

Carduus maria.
Castor equi
Castoreum
Caulophyllum th.
Causticum hannem.
Ceanothus americ.
Cedron
Cepa
Cerium oxalicum
Chamomilla
Chelidonium
Chimaphila umb.
China
Chionantus virg.
Chlorum
Cantharis
Capsicum
Carbo animalis
Carbo vegetabilis

Homeopathy
Table 6

Cinnabaris
Cinnamomum
Cistus canadens.
Clematis
Cobaltum metallicum
Cocculus
Coccus cacti
Coffea
Colchicum
Collinsonia can.
Colocynthis
Condurango
Conium
Convallaria maj.
Crataegus
Crocus
Cicuta virosa
Cimicifuga
Cina

Control Table

Correct
Wishful Thinking
Incorrect

Homeopathy Tables

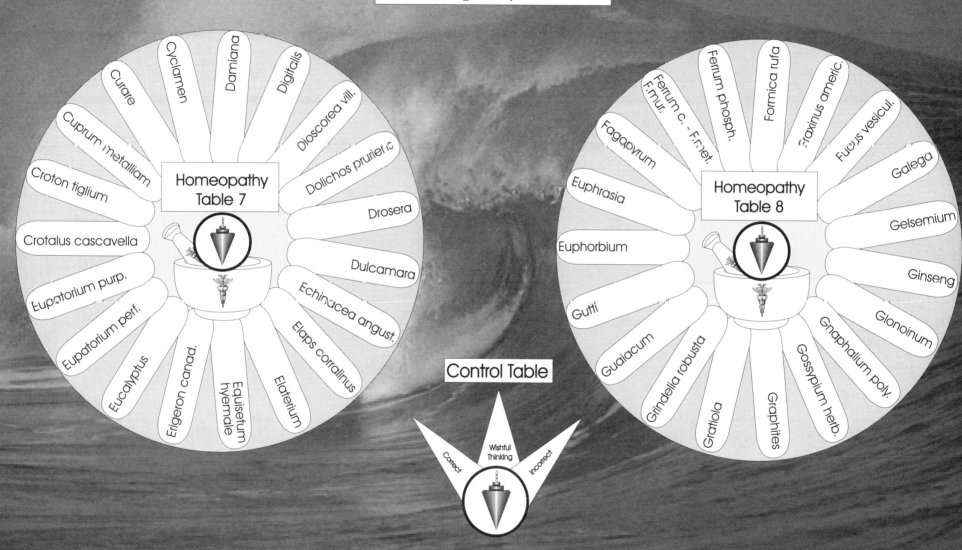

Homeopathy Table 7

- Cyclamen
- Damiana
- Digitalis
- Curare
- Dioscorea vill.
- Cuprum metalliam
- Dolichos pruriet o
- Croton tiglium
- Drosera
- Crotalus cascavella
- Dulcamara
- Eupatorium purp.
- Echinacea angust.
- Eupatorium perf.
- Elaps corralinus
- Eucalyptus
- Erigeron canad.
- Equisetum hyemale
- Elaterium

Homeopathy Table 8

- Ferrum c. - F.net.
- F.mur.
- Ferrum phosph.
- Formica rufa
- Fraxinus americ.
- Fagapyrum
- Fucus vesicul.
- Galega
- Euphrasia
- Gelsemium
- Euphorbium
- Ginseng
- Glonoinum
- Gutti
- Gnaphalium poly.
- Guaiacum
- Gossypium herb.
- Grindelia robusta
- Gratiola
- Graphites

Control Table

- Correct
- Wishful Thinking
- Incorrect

47

Homeopathy Tables

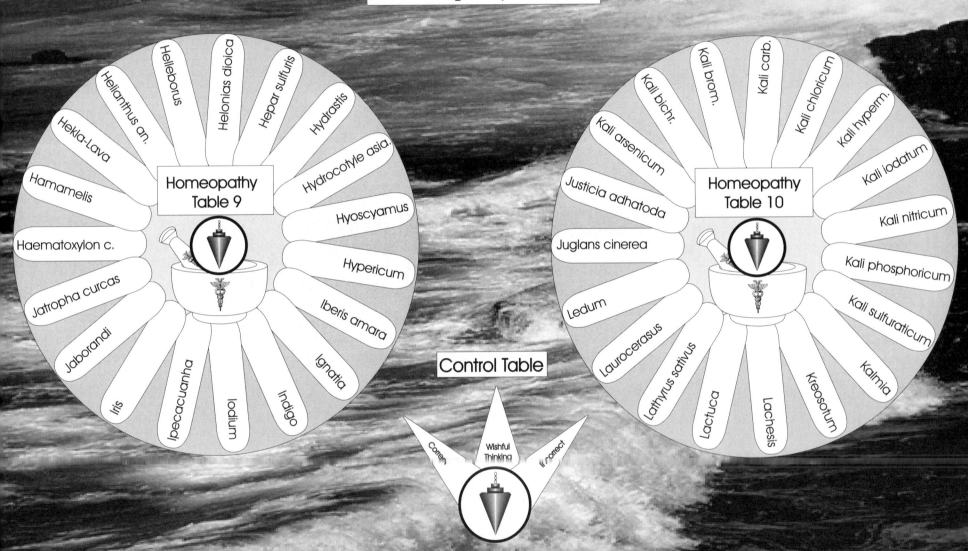

Homeopathy Table 9

- Helleborus
- Helonias dioica
- Hepar sulfuris
- Hydrastis
- Hydrocotyle asia.
- Hyoscyamus
- Hypericum
- Iberis amara
- Ignatia
- Indigo
- Iodium
- Ipecacuanha
- Iris
- Jaborandi
- Jatropha curcas
- Haematoxylon c.
- Hamamelis
- Hekla-Lava
- Helianthus an.

Homeopathy Table 10

- Kali carb.
- Kali chloricum
- Kali hyperm.
- Kali iodatum
- Kali nitricum
- Kali phosphoricum
- Kali sulfuraticum
- Kalmia
- Kreosotum
- Lachesis
- Lactuca
- Lathyrus sativus
- Laurocerasus
- Ledum
- Juglans cinerea
- Justicia adhatoda
- Kali arsenicum
- Kali bichr.
- Kali brom.

Control Table

- Correct
- Wishful Thinking
- Incorrect

48

Homeopathy Tables

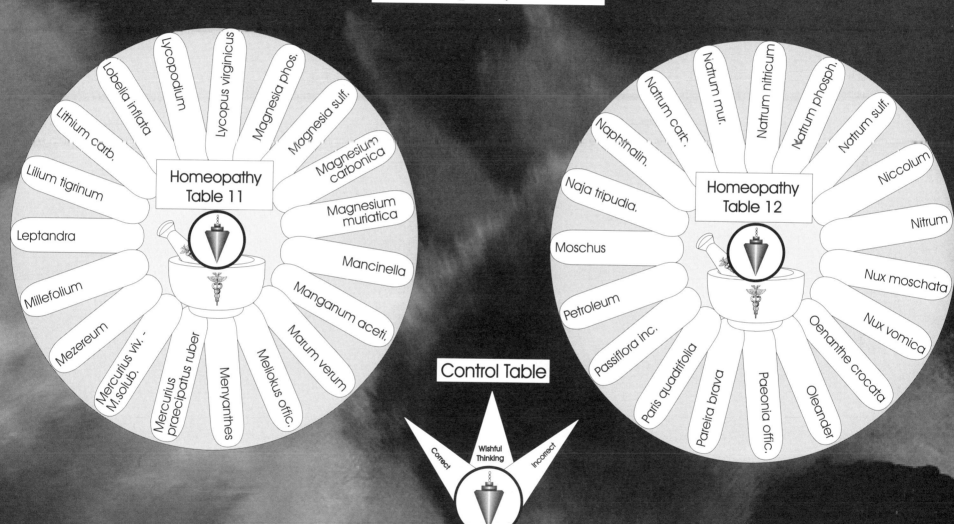

Homeopathy
Table 11

Lycopus virginicus
Lycopodium
Lobelia inflata
Lithium carb.
Lilium tigrinum
Leptandra
Millefolium
Mezereum
Mercurius viv. - M.solub.
Mercurius praecipatus ruber
Menyanthes
Meliokus offic.
Marum verum
Manganum aceti.
Mancinella
Magnesium muriatica
Magnesium carbonica
Magnesia sulf.
Magnesia phos.

Homeopathy
Table 12

Natrum mur.
Natrum nitricum
Natrum phosph.
Natrum carb.
Nattrum sulf.
Naphtalin.
Niccolum
Naja tripudia.
Nitrum
Moschus
Nux moschata
Petroleum
Nux vomica
Passiflora inc.
Oenanthe crocata
Paris quadrifolia
Pareira brava
Paeonia offic.
Oleander

Control Table

Correct
Wishful Thinking
Incorrect

Homeopathy Tables

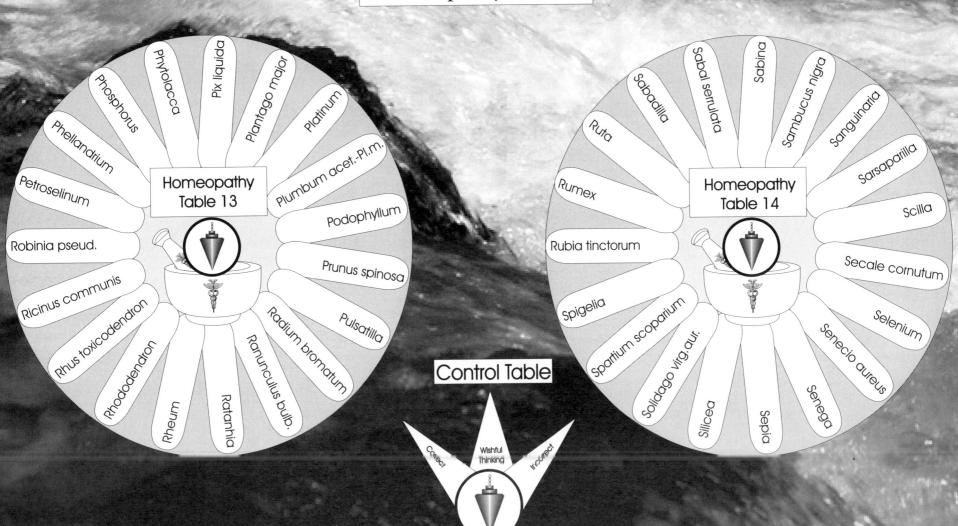

Homeopathy Table 13

Phytolacca, Pix liquida, Plantago major, Platinum, Plumbum acet.-Pl.m., Podophyllum, Prunus spinosa, Pulsatilla, Radium bromatum, Ranunculus bulb., Ratanhia, Rheum, Rhododendron, Rhus toxicodendron, Ricinus communis, Robinia pseud., Petroselinum, Phellandrium, Phosphorus

Homeopathy Table 14

Sabal serrulata, Sabina, Sambucus nigra, Sanguinaria, Sarsaparilla, Scilla, Secale cornutum, Selenium, Senecio aureus, Senega, Sepia, Silicea, Solidago virg. aur., Spartium scoparium, Spigelia, Rubia tinctorum, Rumex, Ruta, Sabadilla

Control Table

Correct, Wishful Thinking, Incorrect

Homeopathy Tables

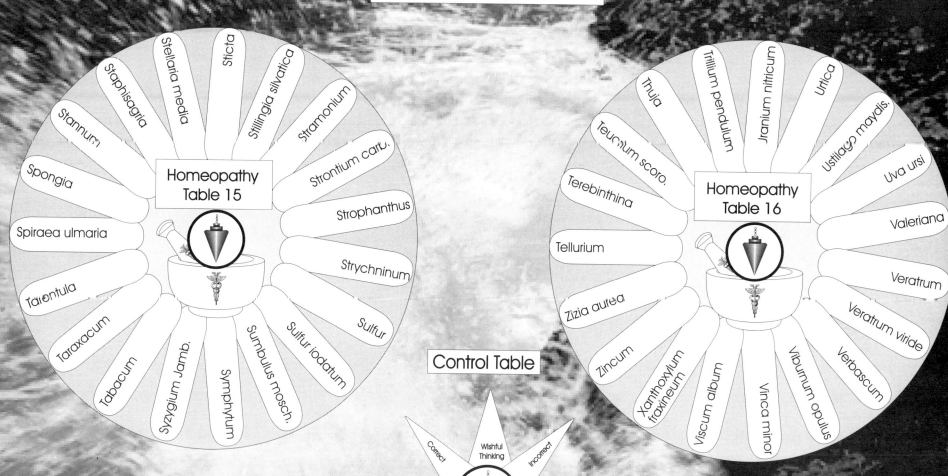

Homeopathy Table 15

- Stellaria media
- Sticta
- Stillingia silvatica
- Staphisagria
- Stramonium
- Stannum
- Strontium carb.
- Spongia
- Strophanthus
- Spiraea ulmaria
- Strychninum
- Tarentula
- Sulfur
- Taraxacum
- Sulfur iodatum
- Tabacum
- Sumbulus mosch.
- Syzygium Jamb.
- Symphytum

Homeopathy Table 16

- Trillium pendulum
- Uranium nitricum
- Thuja
- Urtica
- Teucrium scoro.
- Ustilago maydis.
- Terebinthina
- Uva ursi
- Tellurium
- Valeriana
- Veratrum
- Zizia aurea
- Veratrum viride
- Zincum
- Verbascum
- Xanthoxylum fraxineum
- Viburnum opulus
- Viscum album
- Vinca minor

Control Table

- Correct
- Wishful Thinking
- Incorrect

51

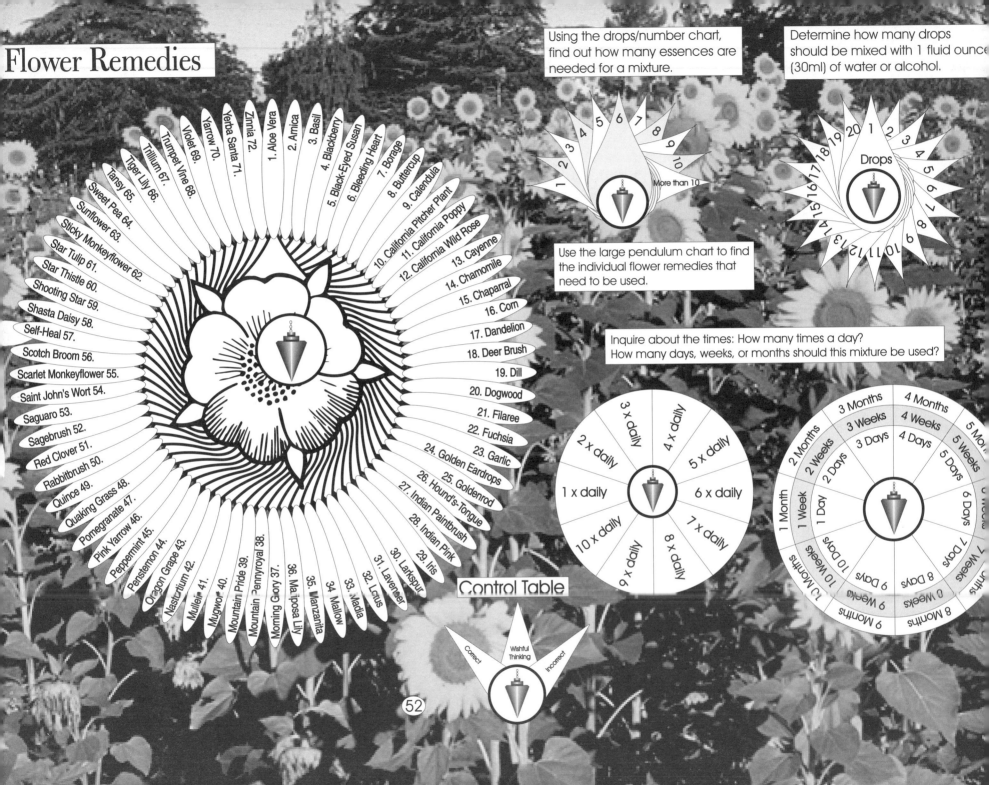

Flower Remedies

Using the drops/number chart, find out how many essences are needed for a mixture.

Determine how many drops should be mixed with 1 fluid ounce (30ml) of water or alcohol.

Use the large pendulum chart to find the individual flower remedies that need to be used.

Inquire about the times: How many times a day? How many days, weeks, or months should this mixture be used?

Flower list:
1. Aloe Vera
2. Arnica
3. Basil
4. Blackberry
5. Black-Eyed Susan
6. Bleeding Heart
7. Borage
8. Buttercup
9. Calendula
10. California Pitcher Plant
11. California Poppy
12. California Wild Rose
13. Cayenne
14. Chamomile
15. Chaparral
16. Corn
17. Dandelion
18. Deer Brush
19. Dill
20. Dogwood
21. Filaree
22. Fuchsia
23. Garlic
24. Golden Eardrops
25. Goldenrod
26. Hound's-Tongue
27. Indian Paintbrush
28. Indian Pink
29. Iris
30. Larkspur
31. Lavender
32. Lotus
33. Madia
34. Mallow
35. Manzanita
36. Mariposa Lily
37. Morning Glory
38. Mountain Pennyroyal
39. Mountain Pride
40. Mugwort
41. Mullein
42. Nasturtium
43. Oregon Grape
44. Penstemon
45. Peppermint
46. Pink Yarrow
47. Pomegranate
48. Quaking Grass
49. Quince
50. Rabbitbrush
51. Red Clover
52. Sagebrush
53. Saguaro
54. Saint John's Wort
55. Scarlet Monkeyflower
56. Scotch Broom
57. Self-Heal
58. Shasta Daisy
59. Shooting Star
60. Star Thistle
61. Star Tulip
62. Sticky Monkeyflower
63. Sunflower
64. Sweet Pea
65. Tansy
66. Tiger Lily
67. Trillium
68. Trumpet Vine
69. Violet
70. Yarrow
71. Yerba Santa
72. Zinnia

Number chart: 1 2 3 4 5 6 7 8 9 10 More than 10

Drops: 1 2 3 4 5 6 7 8 9 10 11 12 13 14 15 16 17 18 19 20

Times chart: 1 x daily, 2 x daily, 3 x daily, 4 x daily, 5 x daily, 6 x daily, 7 x daily, 8 x daily, 9 x daily, 10 x daily

Duration chart: 1 Day, 2 Days, 3 Days, 4 Days, 5 Days, 6 Days, 7 Days, 8 Days, 9 Days, 10 Days, 1 Week, 2 Weeks, 3 Weeks, 4 Weeks, 5 Weeks, 6 Weeks, 7 Weeks, 8 Weeks, 9 Weeks, 10 Weeks, 1 Month, 2 Months, 3 Months, 4 Months, 5 Months, 6 Months, 7 Months, 8 Months, 9 Months, 10 Months, 11 Months, 12 Months

Control Table

Correct, Wishful Thinking, Incorrect

52

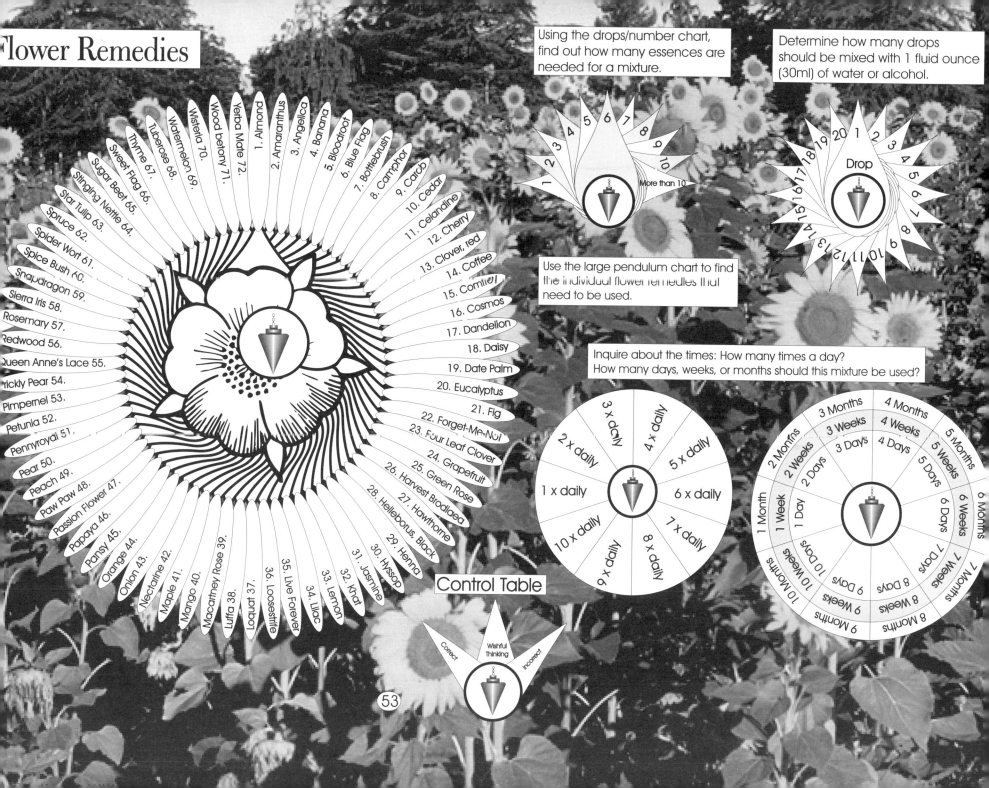

Flower Remedies

Using the drops/number chart, find out how many essences are needed for a mixture.

Determine how many drops should be mixed with 1 fluid ounce (30ml) of water or alcohol.

Use the large pendulum chart to find the individual flower remedies that need to be used.

Inquire about the times: How many times a day? How many days, weeks, or months should this mixture be used?

Control Table

1. Almond
2. Amaranthus
3. Angelica
4. Banana
5. Bloodroot
6. Blue Flag
7. Bottlebrush
8. Camphor
9. Carob
10. Cedar
11. Celandine
12. Cherry
13. Clover, red
14. Coffee
15. Comfrey
16. Cosmos
17. Dandelion
18. Daisy
19. Date Palm
20. Eucalyptus
21. Fig
22. Forget-Me-Not
23. Four Leaf Clover
24. Grapefruit
25. Green Rose
26. Harvest Brodiaea
27. Hawthorne
28. Helleborus, Black
29. Henna
30. Hyssop
31. Jasmine
32. Khat
33. Lemon
34. Lilac
35. Live Forever
36. Loosestrife
37. Loquat
38. Luffa
39. Macartney Rose
40. Mango
41. Maple
42. Nectarine
43. Onion
44. Orange
45. Pansy
46. Papaya
47. Passion Flower
48. Paw Paw
49. Peach
50. Pear
51. Pennyroyal
52. Petunia
53. Pimpernel
54. Prickly Pear
55. Queen Anne's Lace
56. Redwood
57. Rosemary
58. Sierra Iris
59. Snapdragon
60. Spice Bush
61. Spider Wort
62. Spruce
63. Star Tulip
64. Stinging Nettle
65. Sugar Beet
66. Sweet Flag
67. Thyme
68. Tuberose
69. Watermelon
70. Wisteria
71. Wood betony
72. Yerba Mate

1 2 3 4 5 6 7 8 9 10 More than 10

Drop
20 1 2 3 4 5 6 7 8 9 10 11 12 13 14 15 16 17 18 19

3 x daily
4 x daily
2 x daily
5 x daily
1 x daily
6 x daily
10 x daily
7 x daily
9 x daily
8 x daily

3 Months
4 Months
2 Months
3 Weeks
4 Weeks
3 Days
2 Weeks
5 Months
4 Days
5 Weeks
2 Days
3 Days
5 Days
6 Months
1 Month
6 Days
1 Week
6 Weeks
1 Day
7 Days
10 Months
7 Weeks
10 Weeks
8 Days
7 Months
10 Days
9 Days
8 Weeks
9 Weeks
8 Months
9 Months

Correct
Wishful Thinking
Incorrect

53

Bach Flowers

The pendulum wheel contains the following numbered flowers:

1 Agrimony
2 Aspen
3 Beech
4 Centaury
5 Cerato
6 Cherry Plum
7 Chestnut Bud
8 Chicory
9 Clematis
10 Crab Apple
Elm 11
Gentian 12
Gorse 13
Heather 14
Holly 15
Honeysuckle 16
Hornbeam 17
Impatiens 18
Larch 19
Mimulus 20
Mustard 21
Oak 22
Olive 23
Pine 24
Red Chestnut 25
Rock Rose 26
Rock Water 27
Scleranthus 28
Sweet Chestnut 29
Star of Bethlehem 30
31 Vervain
32 Vine
33 Walnut
34 Water Violet
35 White Chestnut
36 Wild Oat
37 Wild Rose
38 Willow
39 Rescue Remedy
40 Rescue with Arnica

Using the drops/number chart, find out how many essences are needed for a mixture.

More than 10

Determine how many drops should be mixed with 1 fluid ounce (30ml) of water or alcohol.

Drops

Use the large pendulum chart to find the individual flower remedies that need to be used.

Inquire about the times: How many times a day? How many days, weeks, or months should this mixture be used?

2 x daily
3 x daily
4 x daily
5 x daily
6 x daily
7 x daily
8 x daily
5 x daily
10 x daily
1 x daily

1 Day
2 Days
3 Days
4 Days
5 Days
6 Days
7 Days
8 Days
9 Days
10 Days
1 Week
2 Weeks
3 Weeks
4 Weeks
5 Weeks
6 Weeks
7 Weeks
8 Weeks
9 Weeks
10 Weeks
1 Month
2 Months
3 Months
4 Months
5 Months
6 Months
7 Months
8 Months
9 Months
10 Months

Control Table

Correct
Wishful thinking
Incorrect

Aromatherapy Oils

How many essential oils should be used?

1 2 3 4 5 6 7 8 9 10 More than 10

On which table is the oil that ought to be used? If more than one, ask about them one after another.

1 2 3 4 5 6

How should the essential oil be used?

Massage oil
Inhalation
Gargling
Compresses
Face care
Skin care

Bath in sitting position
Foot bath
Bath for the whole body
Sea salts for bath
Aroma lamp
Mist
Perfume
Kitchen
Shampoo/Hair care
Night cream
Face cream
Toothpaste
Flower potpourri

Control Table

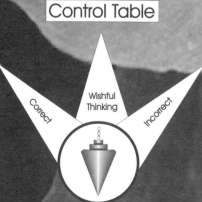

Correct   Wishful Thinking   Incorrect

Is it neccesary to thin the liquid with a base oil?

Yes   No

Which basic oil should be used?

Avocado oil
Apricot core oil
Aloe Vera oil
Almond oil
Calendula oil
Hazelnut oil
Healing earth
Jojoba oil
Night candle oil
Olive oil
Sunflower
Wheat germ oil

55

Aromatherapy Oils

How many drops should be used?
(First question the table on the left
and then the one on the right.)

How much of the basis
oil should I use in
the mixture?

Fluid oz.
Basis Oil

10 13 17 20 24 27 31 34 3 6 68

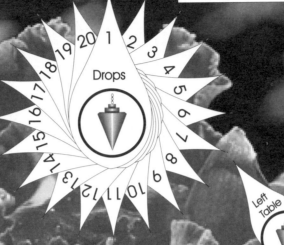

Drops

20 1 2 3 4 5 6 7 8 9 10 11 12 13 14 15 16 17 18 19

Left Table   Right Table

Drops

60 22 24 26 28 30 32 34 36 38 40 42 44 46 48 50 52 54 56 58

Control Table

Correct   Wishful Thinking   Incorrect

How often should the essential
oil mixture be used?

3 x daily   4 x daily   5 x daily   6 x daily   7 x daily   8 x daily   9 x daily   10 x daily   1 x daily   2 x daily

How long should the
essential oil mixture be used?

3 Months   4 Months   5 Months   6 Months   7 Days   8 Days   9 Days   10 Days   7 Weeks   8 Weeks   9 Weeks   10 Weeks   7 Months   8 Months   9 Months   10 Months   1 Month   2 Months   3 Weeks   4 Weeks   5 Weeks   6 Weeks   1 Week   2 Weeks   1 Day   2 Days   3 Days   4 Days   5 Days   6 Days

Aromatherapy Oils

Essential Oil Chart 1

Celery, Chamomile blue, Angelica root, Anise, Asafoetida, Balm, Balm mint, Basil, Bay, Bay leaf, Benzoin, Bergamot, Birch, Blood-orange, Cajeput, Calamus, Camphor, Cananga, Caraway, Cardamon, Carnation blossoms, Carnation leaves, Carrot, Cedar wood

Essential Oil Chart 2

Garlic, Geranium, Chamomile Roman, Cinnamon, Cinnamon bark, Cinnamon leaf, Cistrose galbanum, Citronella, Clementine, Cocoa butter, Coriander, Costus root, Cumin, Cypress, Dill, Douglasie, Dwarf pine, Elemi, Estragon, Eucalyptus, Eucalyptus citridora, Fennel, Fir needle, Galbanum

Control Table

Correct, Wishful Thinking, Incorrect

57

Aromatherapy Oils

Essential Oil Chart 3

Lemon · Lime · Geranium bourbon · Ginger · Lemongrass · Gingergrass · Lemon green · Grapefruit · Lavender fine · Guaiacwood · Lavender extra · Ho-Scho oil · Lavender · Honey · Lavandine · Hops · Larch tree · Immortelle · Kraus mint · Incense · Juniper wood · Iris · Juniper berry · Jasmine

Essential Oil Chart 4

Orange, sweet · Orange, bitter · Oregano · Linalue · Opopanax · Litsea cubeba · Onion · Macis blossom · Ocean Pine · Marjoram · Oak Moss · Meadow Queen · Nutmeg · Mimosa · Niaouli · Mint · Neroli · Mountain bean herb · Narde · Mugwort · Myrtle · Muscatel sage · Myrrh · Musk grains

Control Table

Correct · Wishful Thinking · Incorrect

58

Aromatherapy Oils

Essential Oil Chart 5

Santolin, Sassafras, Silver fir, Palmarosa, Parsley, Patchouli, Pepper, black, Peppermint, Peru balsam, Petitgrain, Pimento, Pine, cembra, Pine, stone, Pine needle, Ravensara (anisata), Rose, Rose (Turkish), Rose (May rose), Rose (Moroccan), Rosemary, Rosewood, Sage, Saint's Wort, Sandalwood

Essential Oil Chart 6

Ylang-Ylang, Ysop, Spearmint, Spike Lavender, St. John's wort, Star anise, Styrax, Tangerine Green, Tangerine Red, Tea Tree, Thuja, Thyme, white, Thyme, red, Tolu, balsam, Tonka, Tuberose, Valerian, Vanilla, Verbena, Vetiver, Violet, White fir, Wintergreen, Yarrow

Control Table

Correct — Wishful Thinking — Incorrect

59

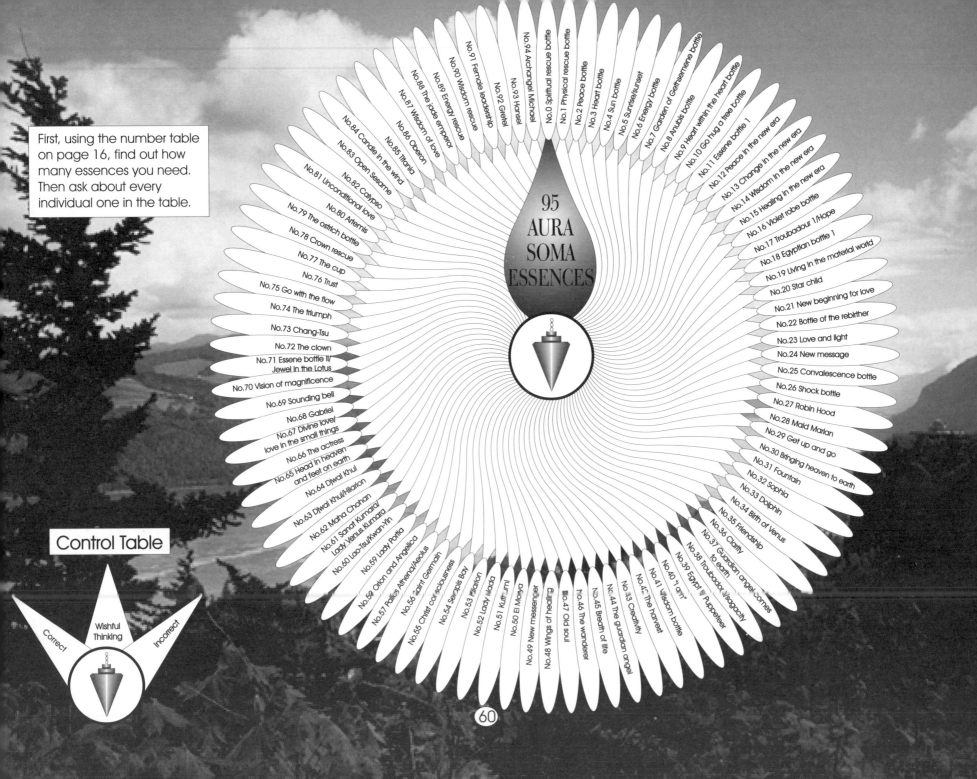

First, using the number table on page 16, find out how many essences you need. Then ask about every individual one in the table.

95 AURA SOMA ESSENCES

Control Table

Correct
Wishful Thinking
Incorrect

No.0 Spiritual rescue bottle
No.1 Physical rescue bottle
No.2 Peace bottle
No.3 Heart bottle
No.4 Sun bottle
No.5 Sunrise/sunset
No.6 Energy bottle
No.7 Garden of Gethsemene bottle
No.8 Anubis bottle
No.9 Heart within the heart bottle
No.10 Go hug a tree bottle
No.11 Essene bottle 1
No.12 Peace in the new era
No.13 Change in the new era
No.14 Wisdom in the new era
No.15 Healing in the new era
No.16 Violet robe bottle
No.17 Troubadour 1/Hope
No.18 Egyptian bottle 1
No.19 Living in the material world
No.20 Star child
No.21 New beginning for love
No.22 Bottle of the rebirther
No.23 Love and light
No.24 New message
No.25 Convalescence bottle
No.26 Shock bottle
No.27 Robin Hood
No.28 Maid Marian
No.29 Get up and go
No.30 Bringing heaven to earth
No.31 Fountain
No.32 Sophia
No.33 Dolphin
No.34 Birth of Venus
No.35 Friendship
No.36 Clarity
No.37 Guardian angel comes to earth
No.38 Troubadour II/Sagacity
No.39 Egypt II/Puppeteer
No.40 "I am"
No.41 Wisdom bottle
No.42 The harvest
No.43 Creativity
No.44 The guardian angel
No.45 Breath of life
No.46 The wanderer
No.47 Old soul
No.48 Wings of healing
No.49 New messenger
No.50 El Morya
No.51 Kuthumi
No.52 Lady Nada
No.53 Hilarion
No.54 Serapis Bay
No.55 Christ consciousness
No.56 Saint Germain
No.57 Pallas Athena/Aeolus
No.58 Orion and Angelica
No.59 Lady Portia
No.60 Lao-Tsu/Kwan-Yin
No.61 Sanat Kumara/Lady Venus Kumara
No.62 Maha Chohan
No.63 Djwal Khul/Hilarion
No.64 Djwal Khul
No.65 Head in heaven and feet on earth
No.66 The actress
No.67 Divine love/love in the small things
No.68 Gabriel
No.69 Sounding bell
No.70 Vision of magnificence
No.71 Essene bottle II/Jewel in the Lotus
No.72 The clown
No.73 Chang-Tsu
No.74 The triumph
No.75 Go with the flow
No.76 Trust
No.77 The cup
No.78 Crown rescue
No.79 The ostrich bottle
No.80 Artemis
No.81 Unconditional love
No.82 Calypso
No.83 Open Sesame
No.84 Candle in the wind
No.85 Titania
No.86 Oberon
No.87 Wisdom of love
No.88 The jade emperor
No.89 Energy rescue
No.90 Wisdom rescue
No.91 Female leadership
No.92 Gretel
No.93 Hansel
No.94 Archangel Michael

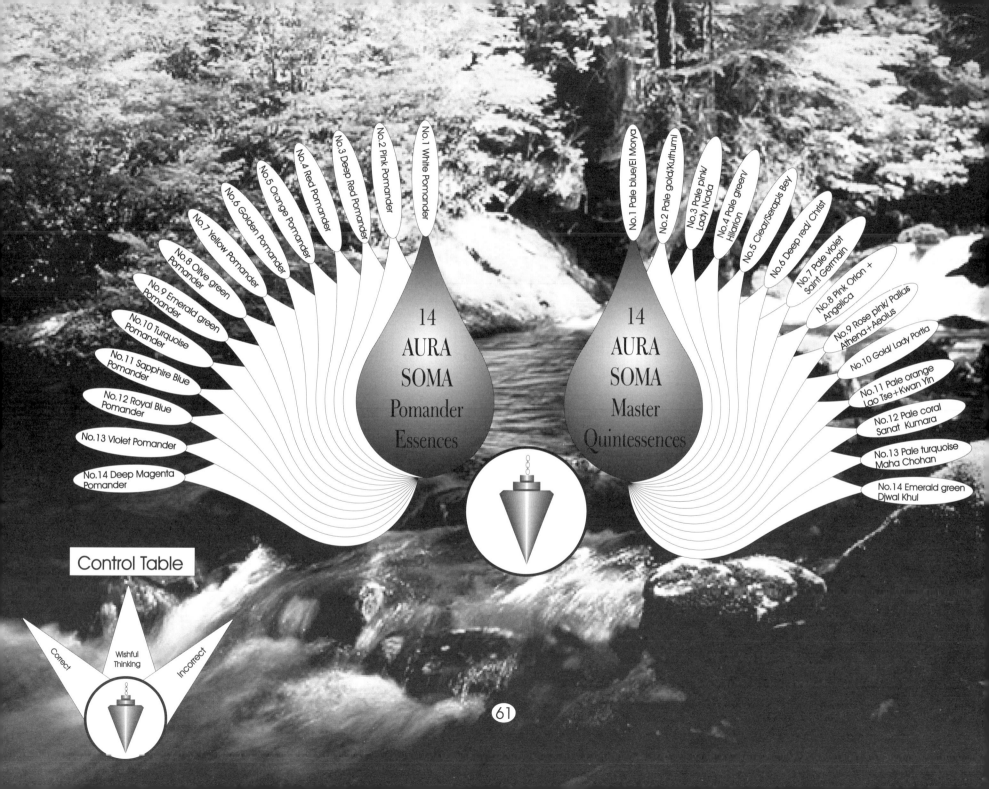

No.1 White Pomander
No.2 Pink Pomander
No.3 Deep Red Pomander
No.4 Red Pomander
No.5 Orange Pomander
No.6 Golden Pomander
No.7 Yellow Pomander
No.8 Olive green Pomander
No.9 Emerald green Pomander
No.10 Turquoise Pomander
No.11 Sapphire Blue Pomander
No.12 Royal Blue Pomander
No.13 Violet Pomander
No.14 Deep Magenta Pomander

14 AURA SOMA Pomander Essences

14 AURA SOMA Master Quintessences

No.1 Pale blue/El Morya
No.2 Pale gold/Kuthumi
No.3 Pale pink/Lady Nada
No.4 Pale green/Hilarion
No.5 Clear/Serapis Bey
No.6 Deep red/Christ
No.7 Pale violet/Saint Germain
No.8 Pink Orion + Angelica
No.9 Rose pink/Pallas Athena+Aeolus
No.10 Gold/Lady Portia
No.11 Pale orange Lao Tse+Kwan Yin
No.12 Pale coral Sanat Kumara
No.13 Pale turquoise Maha Chohan
No.14 Emerald green Djwal Khul

Control Table

Correct
Wishful Thinking
Incorrect

61

Healing Herbs

Left Table **Right Table**

Left Table (herbs)

Acacia, Aconite, Agrimony, Alder, Alfalfa, Allspice, Almond, Aloe vera, Alum, Amaranth, Amber, Angelica, Anise, Arnica, Arrowroot, Asafoetida, Ash, Asparagus, Balm, Barberry, Barley, Basil, Bayberry bark, Bay laurel, Bearberry, Bearsfoot, Belladonna, Benzoin, Bergamot, Betony, Birch, Bistort, Blackberry, Blackthorn, Borage, Brooklime, Bryony, white, Buckhorn, brake, Bugloss, Burdock, Cade, oil of, Caleput, Calamus, Camphor, Capsicum, Caraway, Caroway, Cardamom, Carline Thistle, Carrot, Cascarilla bark, Cassia, Catmint, Cedar, Celandine, Celery, Centaury, Chamomile, Chestnut, Chocolate tree, Christmas Rose, Cinchona, Cimicifuga, Cinnamon, Cinquefoil

Right Table (herbs)

Ivy, Citron, Citronella, Clary Sage, Clematis, Clove, Cohosh, Cottsfoot, Comfrey, Coriander, Cotton root bark, Couch grass, Cowslip, Creosote bush, Cubeb, Daisy, Damiana, Dandelion, Deadly nightshade, Digitalis, Dill, Dragon's blood, Echinacea, Elder, Elecampane, Elm, Ephedra, Ergot, Estragon, Eucalyptus, Evergreen, Eyebright, Fennel, Fenugreek, Feverfew, Filaree, Foxglove, Frankincense, Fuschia, Galanga, Garlic, Gentian, Geranium, Ginger, Ginseng, Goldenrod, Golden seal, Gota Kola, Ground Ivy, wild thyme, Guaiac, Guarana, Gum plant, Hawthorn, Hellebore, Henbane, Hollyhock, Honeysuckle, Hops, Horehound, Horseradish, Horsetail, Hydrangea, Hyssop, Iceland Moss

Control Table

Correct, Wishful Thinking, Incorrect

Since every individual healing herb has to be used in a different way, these pendulum charts can be used only to find the correct plant. In each case, you need to find information elsewhere on how to apply it, consume it, or prepare it—especially since some plants are supposed to be poisonous or not fit to eat. As with all these remedies, be sure to consult your doctor before taking them internally.

Healing Herbs

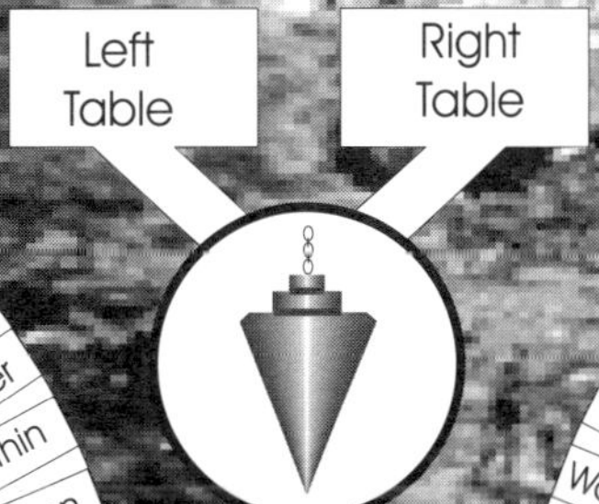

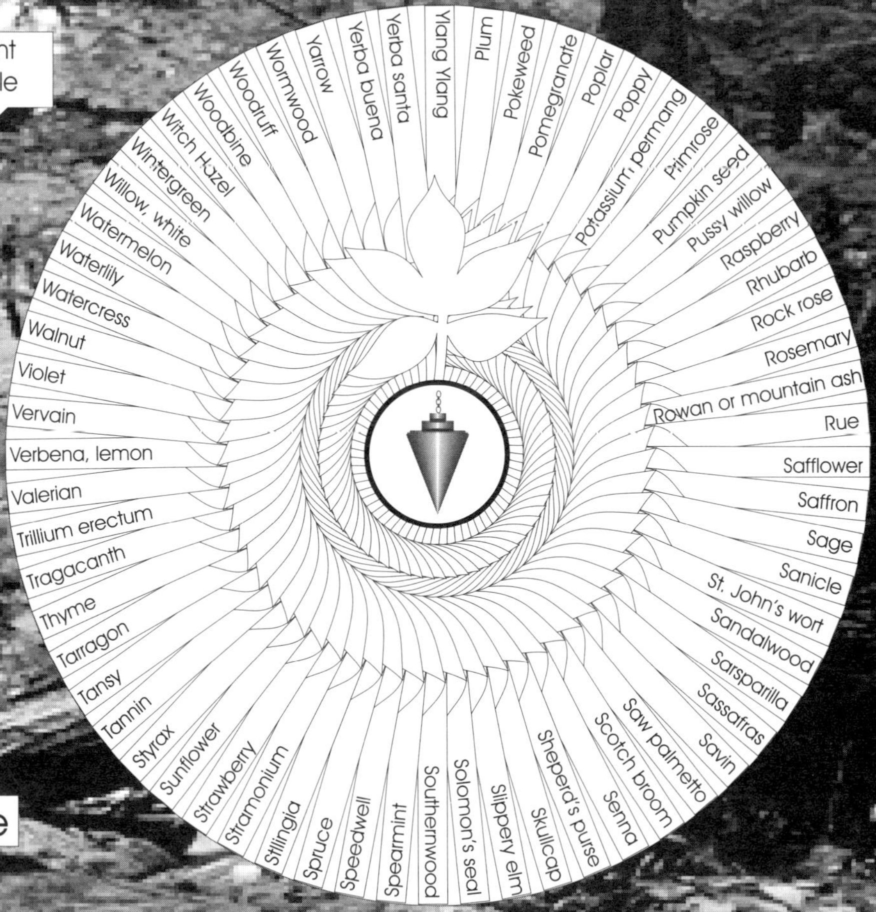

Left Table

Right Table

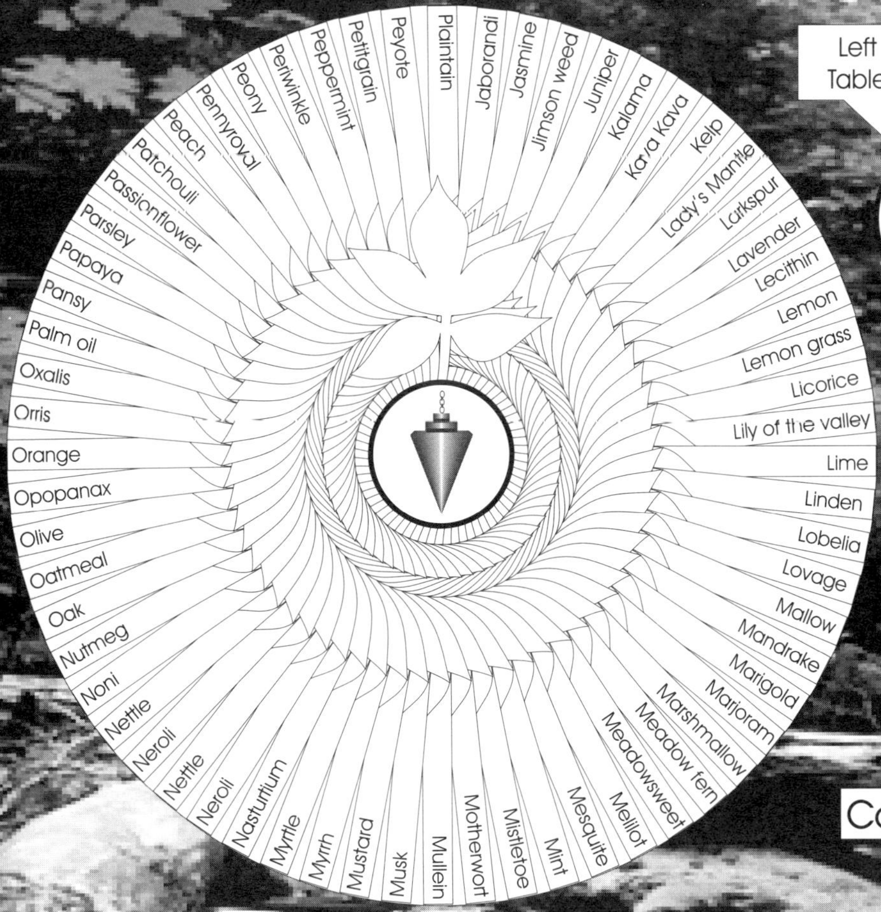

Left Table (herbs):

Peyote, Plaintain, Japanoof, Jasmine, Jimson weed, Juniper, Kalama, Kava Kava, Kelp, Lady's Mantle, Larkspur, Lavender, Lecithin, Lemon, Lemon grass, Licorice, Lily of the valley, Lime, Linden, Lobelia, Lovage, Mallow, Mandrake, Marigold, Marjoram, Marshmallow, Meadow fern, Meadowsweet, Melilot, Mesquite, Mint, Mistletoe, Motherwort, Mullein, Musk, Mustard, Myrrh, Myrtle, Nasturtium, Neroli, Nettle, Nettle, Noni, Nutmeg, Oak, Oatmeal, Olive, Opopanax, Orange, Orris, Oxalis, Palm oil, Pansy, Papaya, Parsley, Passionflower, Patchouli, Peach, Pennyroyal, Peony, Periwinkle, Peppermint, Petitgrain

Right Table (herbs):

Ylang Ylang, Yerba buena, Yerba santa, Yarrow, Wormwood, Woodruff, Woodbine, Witch Hazel, Wintergreen, Willow, white, Watermelon, Waterlily, Watercress, Walnut, Violet, Vervain, Verbena, lemon, Valerian, Trillium erectum, Tragacanth, Thyme, Tarragon, Tansy, Tannin, Styrax, Sunflower, Strawberry, Stramonium, Stillingia, Spruce, Speedwell, Spearmint, Southernwood, Solomon's seal, Slippery elm, Skullcap, Sheperd's purse, Senna, Scotch broom, Saw palmetto, Savin, Sassafras, Sarsparilla, Sandalwood, St. John's wort, Sanicle, Sage, Saffron, Safflower, Rue, Rowan or mountain ash, Rosemary, Rock rose, Rhubarb, Raspberry, Pussy willow, Pumpkin seed, Primrose, Potassium permang, Poppy, Poplar, Pomegranate, Pokeweed, Plum

Control Table

Correct — Wishful Thinking — Incorrect

Since every individual healing herb has to be used in a different way, these pendulum charts can be used only to find the correct plant. In each case, you need to find information on how to apply it, consume it, or prepare it—especially since some plants are supposed to be poisonous or not fit to eat. Be sure to consult your doctor before taking any of these herbs internally.

63

Chinese Healing Herbs and Plants

Since every individual healing herb has to be used in a different way, these pendulum charts can be used only to find the correct plant. In each case, you need to find information on how to apply it, consume it, or prepare it—especially since some plants are supposed to be poisonous or not fit to eat. Be sure to consult your doctor before raking any of these herbs internally.

Control Table

Correct   Wishful Thinking   Incorrect

Safflower
Rose
Self-heal
Sesame
Snake Bed Seed
Sweet Apricot
Wild asparagus
Acanthopanax root
Agrimony
Angelica
Asian Dandelion
Asiatic plantain
Asiatic plaintain seed
Bitter Apricot
Black false hellebore
Chinese clematis
Chinese hawthorn
Chinese magnolia vine fruits
Chinese pulsatilla
Chinese wild ginger
Chinese yam
Cockscomb
Coin grass
Costus root
Dodder seed
Eucommia bark
Evodia
Ginseng
Gorgon fruit
Hare's ear
Herb of colored mistletoe
Japanese honeysuckle
Korean mint
Jujube
Licorice
Lotus flower
Medicinal Cornel Fruit
Monkshood
Morinda Root
Mulberry leaved chrysanthemum
Oriental Arborvitae Seed
Pseudoginsend
Purple aster
Purple sage
Red peony root
Rhubarb
Root of Chinese ephedra
Root of lobed kudzu vine

Native American Healing Herbs and Plants

Since every individual healing herb has to be used in a different way, these pendulum charts can be used only to find the correct plant. In each case, you need to find information on how to apply it, consume it, or prepare it—especially since some plants are supposed to be poisonous or not fit to eat. Be sure to consult your doctor before taking any of these herbs internally.

Control Table

Correct   Wishful Thinking   Incorrect

Wild yarm root, Willow, red, Wood betony, Wormwood, Yellow cock, Yerba scnta, Alfalfa, Aloe Vera, Angelica, Arrowwood, Barberry, Bearberry, Birch, Black cohosh, Black walnut, Burdock, Cascara sagrada, Catnip, Cedar, Chaparral, Cherry, Chickweed, Coltsfoot, Corn/cornsilk, Dandelion, Deers tongue, Devil's club, Dong quai, Echinacea, Elderberry, Ephedra, Eucalyptus, Garlic, Ginger, Ginseng, Golden seal, Hawthorne berry, Juniper, Kava kava, Lady's Slipper, Lambsquarter, Laurel, Licorice, Lobelia, Milkweed, Mesquite, Mullein, Oregon grape root, Peppermint leaves, Pinon, Polkweed, Poplar, Pumpkin seeds, Red clover, Sage, Sarsparilla, Saw palmetto, Senna, Skullcap, Slippery elm, St. John's wort, Sumac leaves, Squaw bush, Sweet grass, Tobacco, Uva ursa, Valerian, Wild lettuce, Wild onions

Tea Tables

On which tea table will I find the right kind?

Tea Table 1
Tea Table 2
Tea Table 3
Tea Table 4

How long should the tea brew?

5 Minutes
7 Minutes
10 Minutes
15 Minutes
20 Minutes
3 Minutes
30 Minutes

How many kinds of tea shall the mixture contain?

1 2 3 4 5 6 7 8 9 10

How many times a day should the tea be taken?

1x 2x 3x 4x 5x

How many grams do I need for ¼ liter of water?

5 Grams
10 Grams
15 Grams
20 Grams
25 Grams
30 Grams
35 Grams

Control Table

Correct
Wishful Thinking
Incorrect

How long should the tea be taken?

1 Day
2 Days
3 Days
4 Days
5 Days
1 week
2 weeks
3 weeks
4 weeks
5 weeks

66

Tea Table

Tea Table 1

Camellia, Caraway, Carrot, Catnip, Agrimony, Alder, Alfalfa, Angelica, Anise, Apple, Arnica, Balm, Barberry, Basil, Bay, Bearberry, Bergamot, Betony, Birch, Blackberry, Bladderwrack, Blue Flag (American Swamp Iris), Borage, Buchu, Burdock, Calamint

Tea Table 2

Garlic, Gentian, Geranium, Ginger, Celery, Centaury, Chamomile, Chervil, Chestnut, Chickweed, Chicory root, Cinnamon, Coltsfoot, Comfrey, Coriander, Cornsilk, Costmary, Couch grass, Cumin, Daisy, Dandelion, Elder, Fennel, Fenugreek, Feverfew, Flax

Control Table

Correct, Wishful Thinking, Incorrect

67

Tea Tables

Tea Table 3

Goldenrod herb
Ginseng
Orange
Nettle
Myrrh
Mustard, White
Mullein
Mugwort
Mint
Marshmallow
Marjoram
Marigold
Lungwort
Lovage
Lime
Licorice
Lemon
Lavender
Juniper
Jasmine
Hyssop
Hops
Hemp seed
Heather
Hawthorn
Hawkweed

Tea Table 4

Yarrow
Parsley
Passion Flower
Peppermint
Pipsissewa
Plantain
Primrose
Raspberry
Rose
Rosehips
Rosemary
Rowan
Sage
Sandalwood
Sarsparilla
Scarlet Pimpernel
Skullcap
Sorrel
St. John's Wort
Tarragon
Thyme
Valerian
Vervain
Walnut
Watercress
Wormwood

Control Table

Correct
Wishful Thinking
Incorrect

68

What part should be used?

- Blossoms
- Leaves/needles
- Seeds
- Wood/branches
- Essential oil
- Buds
- Wood
- Bark
- Fruits

How should it be used?

- Hug it
- As a compress
- Rubbing in
- In a bath
- Powder/spice
- As an ointment
- Tincture
- Burning/smudging
- Tea
- Washing
- Meditation
- Rubbing off
- As a food

Control Table

- Correct
- Wishful Thinking
- Incorrect

Tree Table

- Willow
- Yew
- Alder
- Apple
- Ash
- Barberry
- Beech
- Birch
- Boxtree
- Cedar
- Cherry
- Chestnut
- Cypress
- Elder
- Elm
- Fir (silver)
- Fir (spruce)
- Hawthorn
- Hazelnut
- Hornbeam
- Juniper
- Larch
- Laurel/bay
- Lilac
- Lime
- Maple
- Oak
- Pear
- Pine, Scotch
- Pine, Stone
- Plum
- Quince
- Rowan/Mountain ash
- Sloe tree/Black-thorn
- Thuja
- Walnut

Burning and Smudging with Resins, Balsams, and Woods

Control Table

Correct   Wishful Thinking   Incorrect

Tolu-Balsam
Aloe
Asphalt
Turpentine resins
Asafoetida (Devil's dung)
Benzoin-Siam
Benzoin Sumatra
Styrax
Sandalwood, white
Sandalwood, red
Cascarilla
Camphor
Sweet-grass
Cedar (wood)
Opoponax
Cinnamon
Sage
Cypress (wood)
Mastix
Myrrh
Elder
Kopal
Frankincense
Kalmia
Galanga
Dragon's blood
Incense
Juniper (wood)
Hickory
Ginseng

70

Identifying Zones of Disturbance

Rejection

Rejection (intersection)

Global grid

Global grid/Crossing

Crossing/Intersection

Place that is free of rays/radiation

Water

Water/ Crossing

Water/ Rejection

Water/ Intersection

Intersection

Control Table

Correct

Wishful Thinking

Incorrect

Intensity of the Rays

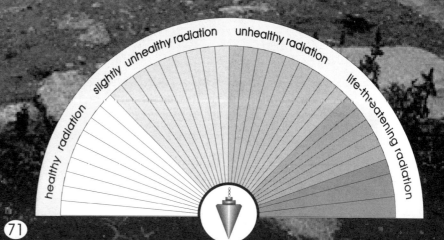

healthy radiation

slightly unhealthy radiation

unhealthy radiation

life-threatening radiation

71

Intensity of Energy

a) Intensity of earth rays/places

b) Energetic vital radiation of human beings

c) Intensity of radiation in food supplies

Which circle should be used?

Middle/1st Circle
Inner/1st Circle
Outer/3rd Circle

Control Table

Correct
Wishful Thinking
Incorrect

Inner Pendulum circle (physical)

This circle will let you know the intensity of the radiation in a place, as well as the vibrations that have a direct influence on human beings.

0-2000 BU	Intersection of 2 or more disturbance zones; disturbance because of a defense mechanism or such growth disturbances as cancer
2000-6000 BU	Damaging disturbance zone for the human organism
6500 BU	Neutral
7000-8000 BU	Best value/full vitality
9000-10,000 BU	Too high, in the long run

Middle Pendulum circle (ethereal-spiritual)

10,000-13,500 BU	Energetic or ethereal area of the body
13,500-18,000 BU	Spiritual and metaphysical area: sacred and sacral sites, up to sacred initiation places, such as the pyramids and Stonehenge

Outer pendulum circle:

from 18,000 BU	Cosmic ray/fields

BU = Bovis units

Water Tables for Locating Underground Sources

Control Table

Correct · Wishful Thinking · Incorrect

Water Movement in Liters per Minute

0 Liters
100 Liters
200 Liters
300 Liters
400 Liters
500 Liters
600 Liters
700 Liters
800 Liters
900 Liters
1000 Liters
1100 Liters
1200 Liters
1300 Liters
1400 Liters
1500 Liters
1600 Liters
1700 Liters
1800 Liters

Depth of Water in Meters

0 m
5 m
10 m
15 m
20 m
25 m
30 m
35 m
40 m
45 m
50 m
55 m
60 m
65 m
70 m
75 m
80 m
85 m
90 m
95 m
100 m
105 m
110 m
115 m
120 m
125 m
130 m
135 m
140 m
145 m
150 m
155 m
160 m
165 m
170 m
175 m
180 m

Water Tables for Locating Underground Sources

Control Table

Correct

Wishful Thinking

Incorrect

Water Hardness in Degrees
Hardest/Softest

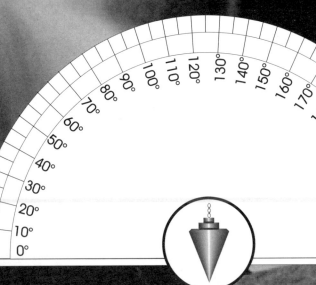

Water Temperature

0°Celsius 32°F
10°Celsius 50°F
20°Celsius 70°F
30° Celsius 90°F
40°Celsius 110°F
50°Celsius 125°F
60°Celsius 137°F
70°Celsius 150°F
80° Celsius 175°F
90°Celsius 200° F
100°Celsius 212°F

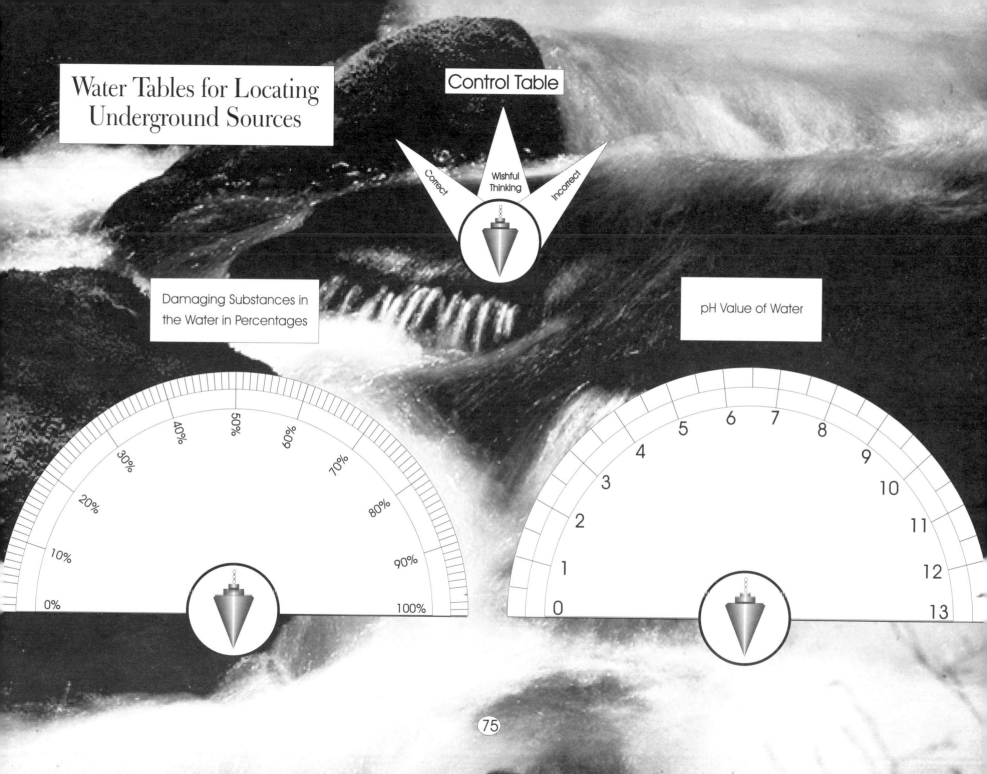

Water Tables for Locating Underground Sources

Control Table

Correct
Wishful Thinking
Incorrect

Damaging Substances in the Water in Percentages

pH Value of Water

Gemstones and Minerals

Control Table

- Correct
- Wishful Thinking
- Incorrect

Which chart is the right one to use?

1
2
3
4
5
6
7
8

Cleaning and/or Activating the Gemstones

- Cleaning them mentally
- Holding them under running water
- No cleaning necessary
- Placing them among crystals
- Placing them in salt water
- Placing them in sand
- Placing them in the earth
- Placing them in the sun
- Placing them under a pyramid
- Through breathing
- Through burning or smudging
- Through sounds
- With prayers or with meditations

Form of the Stones

- Ring
- Cabuchon
- Chain/ball or ellipse
- Chain or necklace/chip
- Cylinder stone
- Egg or ball
- Facetted stone
- Healing wand
- Natural pyramid
- Pendant (different shapes)
- Pendant, doughnut
- Pyramid, cube or obelisk
- Raw

76

Gemstones and Minerals

Control Table

- Correct
- Wishful Thinking
- Incorrect

How should the gemstone be used?

- Wearing around the neck
- As a transmitter
- As protection stone
- Carrying with you in a pouch
- For clearing (cleansing) of rooms
- For energizing
- For meditation
- For stroking meridians
- In reflexology
- Laying on
- Placing underneath or beside the bed
- Taking (in a gemstone elixir)
- To convey messages

On which part of the body should the gemstone be used?

- Additional center: feet
- 1. Chakra genital area
- 2. Chakra loin area
- 3. Chakra waist area
- 4. Chakra chest area
- 5. Chakra neck area
- 6. Chakra forehead area
- 7. Chakra crown of head area
- 8. Chakra enhanced Kundalini
- Additional center: hands
- Additional center:

How long should the gemstone be used?

- 4 Months
- 3 Months
- 3 Weeks
- 3 Days
- 2 Months
- 2 Weeks
- 2 Days
- 1 Month
- 1 Week
- 1 Day
- 10 Months
- 10 Weeks
- 10 Days
- 9 Months
- 9 Weeks
- 9 Days
- 8 Months
- 8 Weeks
- 8 Days
- 7 Months
- 7 Weeks
- 7 Days
- 4 Weeks
- 4 Days
- 5 Months
- 5 Weeks
- 5 Days
- 6 Months
- 6 Weeks
- 6 Days

How often should the gemstone be used?

- 3 x daily
- 4 x daily
- 5 x daily
- 6 x daily
- 7 x daily
- 8 x daily
- 9 x daily
- Hourly
- 1 x daily
- 2 x daily

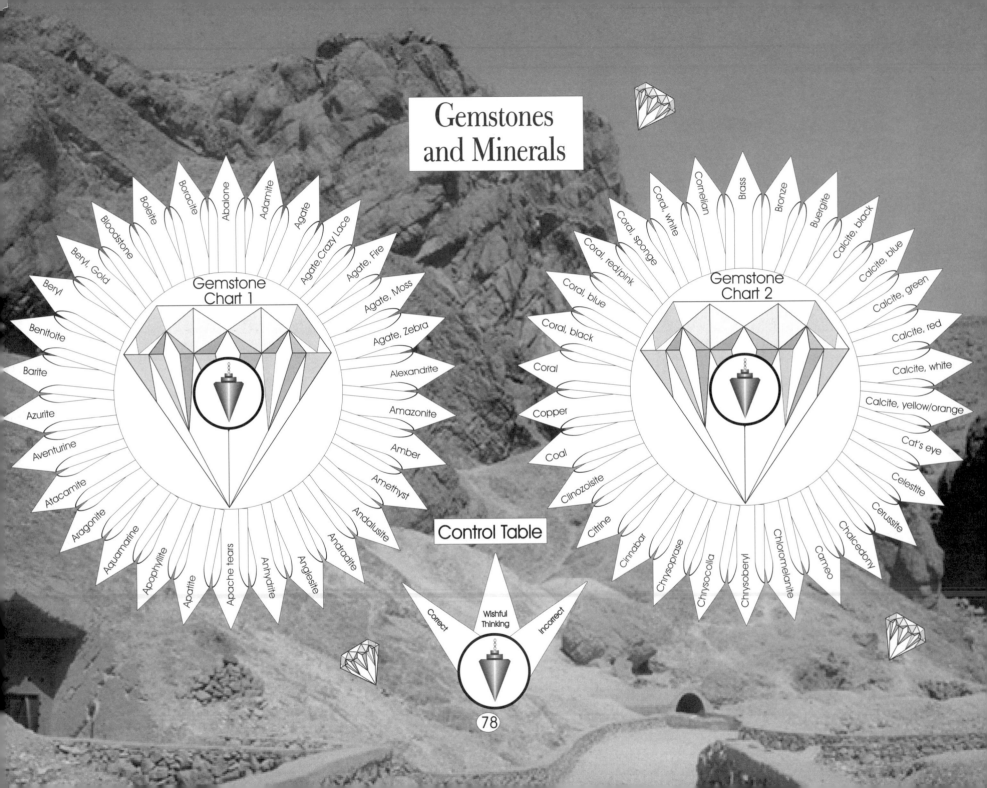

Gemstones and Minerals

Gemstone Chart 1

Adamite
Abalone
Boracite
Boleite
Bloodstone
Beryl, Gold
Beryl
Benitoite
Barite
Azurite
Aventurine
Atacamite
Aragonite
Aquamarine
Apophyllite
Apatite
Apache tears
Anhydrite
Anglesite
Andradite
Andalusite
Amethyst
Amber
Amazonite
Alexandrite
Agate, Zebra
Agate, Moss
Agate, Fire
Agate, Crazy Lace
Agate

Gemstone Chart 2

Cornelian
Brass
Bronze
Coral, white
Buergite
Coral, sponge
Calcite, black
Coral, red/pink
Calcite, blue
Coral, blue
Calcite, green
Coral, black
Calcite, red
Coral
Calcite, white
Copper
Calcite, yellow/orange
Coal
Cat's eye
Clinozoisite
Celestite
Citrine
Cerussite
Cinnabar
Chalcedony
Chrysoprase
Cameo
Chrysocolla
Chloromelanite
Chrysoberyl

Control Table

Correct
Wishful Thinking
Incorrect

78

Gemstones and Minerals

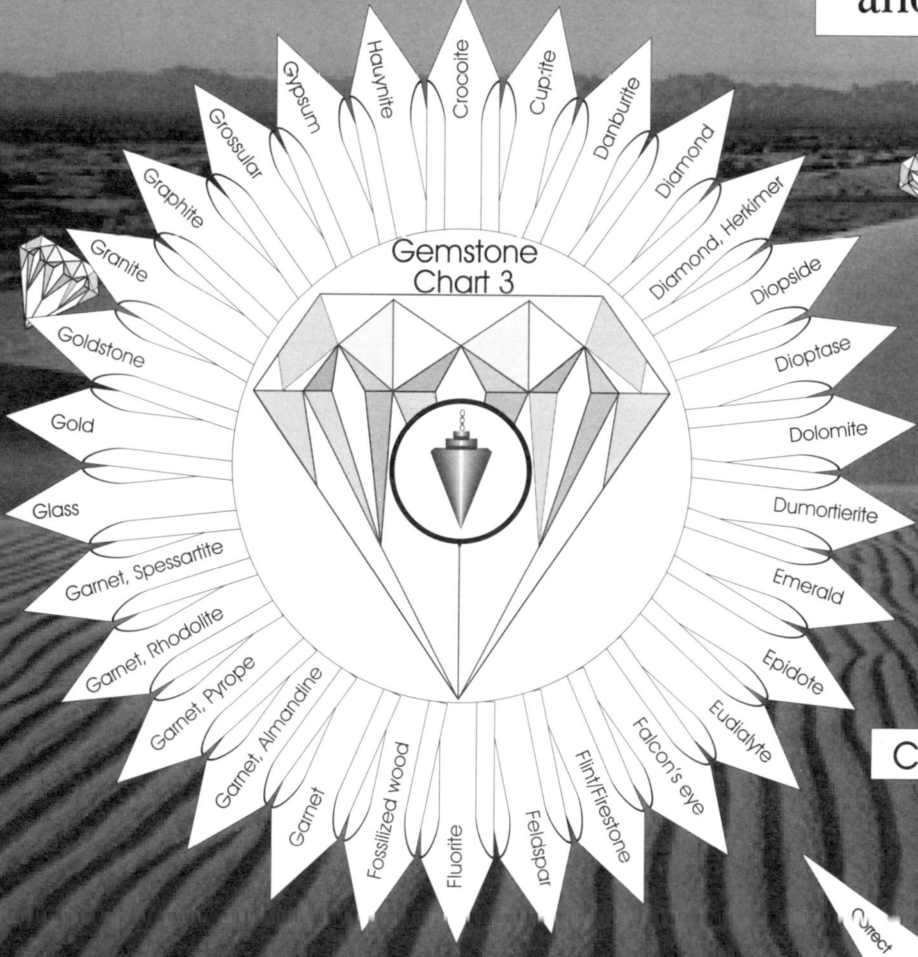

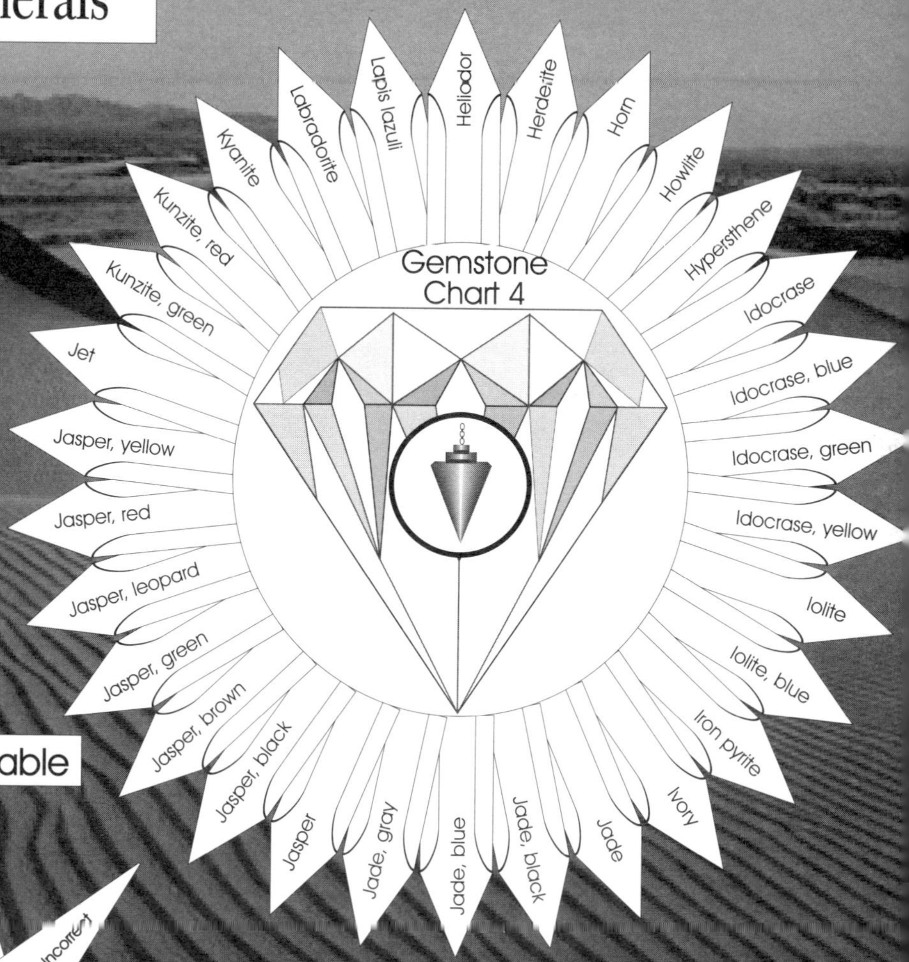

Gemstone Chart 3

- Gypsum
- Hauynite
- Crocoite
- Cupirte
- Danburite
- Diamond
- Diamond, Herkimer
- Diopside
- Dioptase
- Dolomite
- Dumortierite
- Emerald
- Epidote
- Eudialyte
- Falcon's eye
- Flint/Firestone
- Feldspar
- Fluorite
- Fossilized wood
- Garnet
- Garnet, Almandine
- Garnet, Pyrope
- Garnet, Rhodolite
- Garnet, Spessartite
- Glass
- Gold
- Goldstone
- Granite
- Graphite
- Grossular

Gemstone Chart 4

- Kyanite
- Labradorite
- Lapis lazuli
- Heliodor
- Herderite
- Horn
- Howlite
- Hypersthene
- Idocrase
- Idocrase, blue
- Idocrase, green
- Idocrase, yellow
- Iolite
- Iolite, blue
- Iron pyrite
- Ivory
- Jade
- Jade, black
- Jade, blue
- Jade, gray
- Jasper
- Jasper, black
- Jasper, brown
- Jasper, green
- Jasper, leopard
- Jasper, red
- Jasper, yellow
- Jet
- Kunzite, green
- Kunzite, red

Control Table

- Correct
- Wishful Thinking
- Incorrect

79

Gemstones and Minerals

Gemstone Chart 5

- Opal, fire
- Opal, white
- Lazulite
- Legrandite
- Lepidolite
- Leucite
- Ludlamite
- Magnetite
- Malachite
- Marble
- Marcasite
- Mesolite
- Meteorite
- Milarite
- Milk Opal
- Moldavite
- Moonstone
- Mother-of-Pearl
- Moukaite
- Muscovite
- Natrolite
- Neptunite
- Obsidian
- Obsidian, black
- Obsidian, gold
- Obsidian, rainbow
- Obsidian, snowflake
- Onyx
- Opal
- Opal, black

Gemstone Chart 6

- Ruby
- Rutile
- Sapphire
- Opaline
- Orthoclase
- Padparadscha x
- Pearl
- Pearl, black
- Pearl, freshwater
- Periclase
- Peridot
- Phosgenite
- Platinum
- Prase
- Prasiolite
- Prehnite
- Proustite
- Purpurite
- Pyrite
- Pyrolusite
- Quartz
- Quartz, clear
- Quartz, emerald
- Quartz, rose
- Quartz, sapphire
- Quartz, smoky
- Quartz, star
- Rhodochrosite
- Rhodonite
- Rock crystal

Control Table

- Correct
- Wishful Thinking
- Incorrect

80

Gemstones and Minerals

Gemstone Chart 7

Tiger's iron · Tin · Sard · Selenite · Serpentine · Siderite · Silver · Sodalite · Spectrolite · Spinel · Spinel, black · Spinel, blue · Spinel, green · Spinel, red/pink · Spinel, white/transparent · Spinel, yellow · Staurolite · Stellerite · Stichtite · Strontianite · Sugilite · Sulphur · Sunstone · Sunstone, blue · Sunstone, clear · Sunstone, green · Sunstone, pink · Tanzanite · Tektite · Tiger's eye

Gemstone Chart 8

Zoisite · Topaz · Topaz, blue · Topaz, clear · Topaz, gold · Topaz, green · Topaz, pink · Topaz, white · Torbernite · Tourmaline · Tourmaline, black · Tourmaline, blue · Tourmaline, brown · Tourmaline, green · Tourmaline, rainbow · Tourmaline, red/pink · Tourmaline, yellow · Turquoise · Ulexite · Vanadinite · Vesuvianite · Vivianite · Wulfenite · Zinc blende · Zincite · Zircon · Zircon, blue · Zircon, green · Zircon, pink/red · Zircon, yellow

Control Table

Correct · Wishful Thinking · Incorrect

81

Weather Forecasting

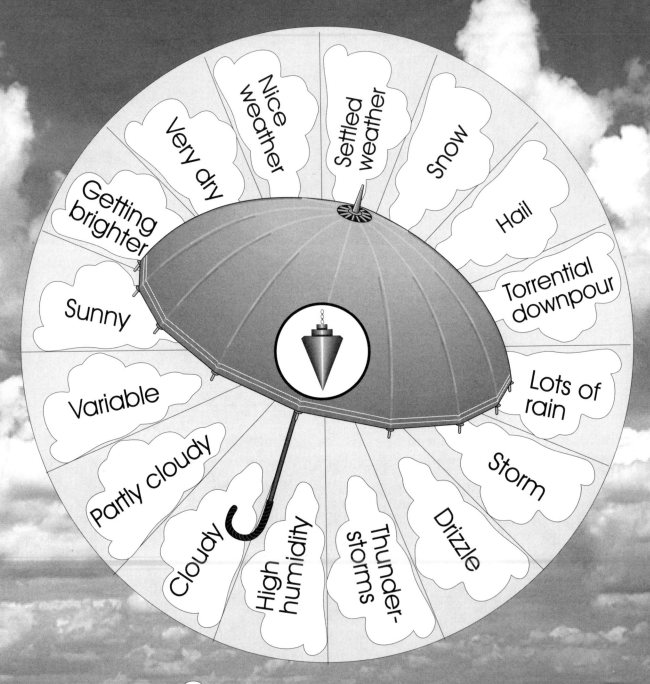

Nice weather

Settled weather

Snow

Very dry

Hail

Getting brighter

Torrential downpour

Sunny

Lots of rain

Variable

Storm

Partly cloudy

Cloudy

High humidity

Thunder-storms

Drizzle

Control Table

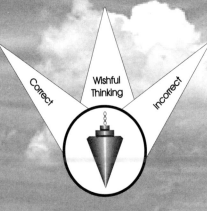

Correct

Wishful Thinking

Incorrect

The Medicine Wheel

Totem Animals

Control Table

Correct · Wishful Thinking · Incorrect

Ant · Antelope · Armadillo · Badger · Bat · Bear · Beaver · Buffalo · Butterfly · Coyote · Crow · Doe · Dog · Dolphin · Dragonfly · Eagle · Elk · Falcon · Fox · Frog · Hare · Hawk · Horse · Lizard · Lynx · Mountain Lion · Mouse · Opossum · Otter · Owl · Porcupine · Prairie chicken · Rattlesnake · Raven · Skunk · Snake · Spider · Squirrel · Swan · Turkey · Turtle · Weasel · Whale · Wolf

Runes
Viking Runes

Control Table

Correct · Wishful Thinking · Incorrect

1. FEOH
2. UR
3. THORN
4. ANSUR
5. RAD
6. KEN
7. HAGALL
8. NIED
9. IS
10. JARA
11. SIGEL
12. TIR
13. BEORC
14. LAGU
15. MANN
16. YR
17. EOH
18. OTHEL

Air
ASGARD
Fog
Fire
N
MID
O
Water
Fire
GARD
W
S
Fountain
Volcano
UTGARD
Earth

Runes
Common Runes

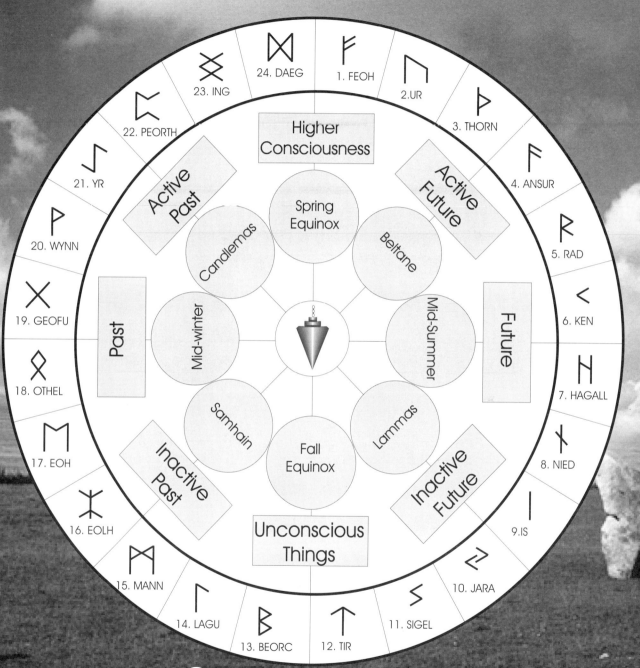

Higher Consciousness

Active Past

Active Future

Past

Future

Inactive Past

Inactive Future

Unconscious Things

Spring Equinox

Candlemas

Beltane

Mid-winter

Mid-Summer

Samhain

Lammas

Fall Equinox

1. FEOH
2. UR
3. THORN
4. ANSUR
5. RAD
6. KEN
7. HAGALL
8. NIED
9. IS
10. JARA
11. SIGEL
12. TIR
13. BEORC
14. LAGU
15. MANN
16. EOLH
17. EOH
18. OTHEL
19. GEOFU
20. WYNN
21. YR
22. PEORTH
23. ING
24. DAEG

Control Table

Correct

Wishful Thinking

Incorrect

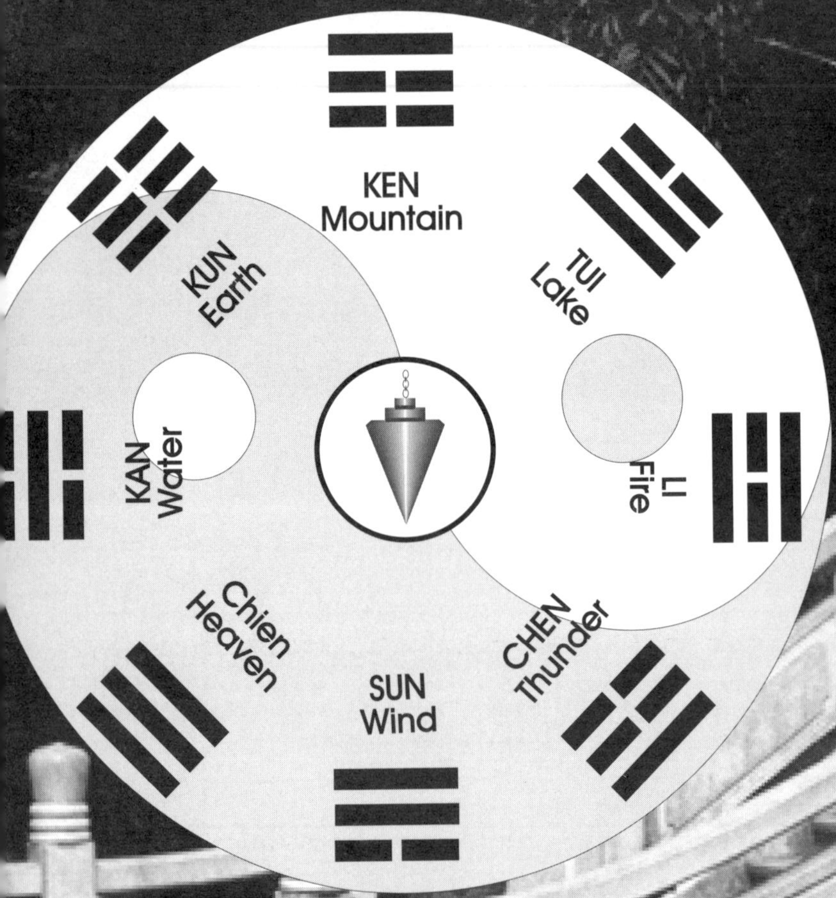

I Ching Oracle

KEN Mountain

TUI Lake

KUN Earth

LI Fire

KAN Water

Chien Heaven

SUN Wind

CHEN Thunder

1. With the help of the chart on the left, first swing the pendulum to determine the lower trigram, and then the upper one. With the table on the right, you can now find the number of the hexagram.

2. Using the lower left table, ask how many lines move. Then ask which line/s change on the right.

UPPER TRIGRAM ▷ / LOWER TRIGRAM ▽	CHEIN	CHEN	KAN	KEN	KUN	SUN	LI	TUI
CHIEN	1	34	5	26	11	9	14	43
CHEN	25	51	3	27	24	42	21	17
KAN	6	40	29	4	7	59	64	47
KEN	33	62	39	52	15	53	56	31
KUN	12	16	8	23	2	20	35	45
SUN	44	32	48	18	46	57	50	28
LI	13	55	63	22	36	37	30	49
TUI	10	54	60	41	19	61	38	58

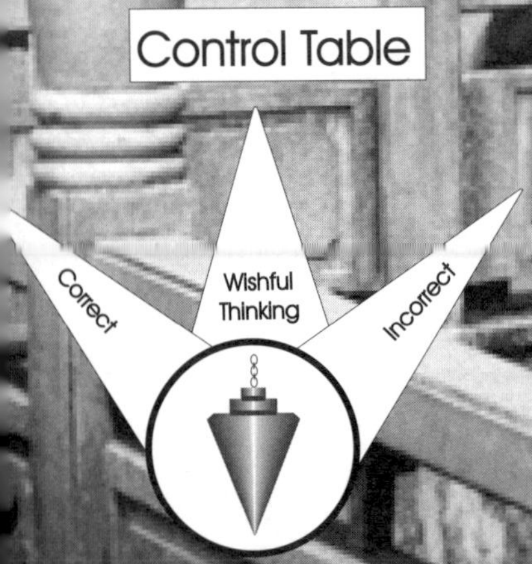

Control Table

Correct / Wishful Thinking / Incorrect

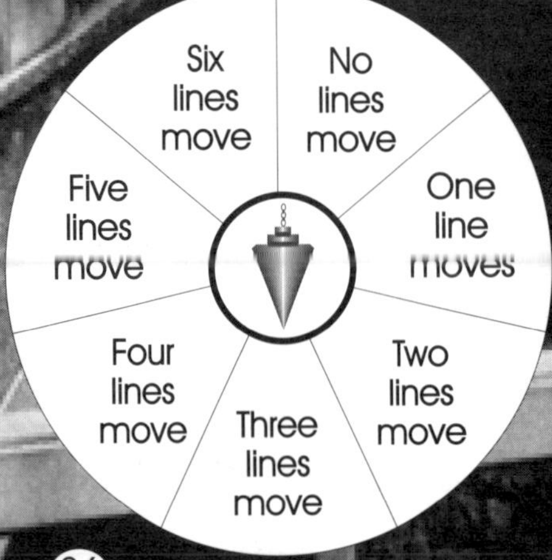

Six lines move / No lines move / Five lines move / One line moves / Four lines move / Three lines move / Two lines move

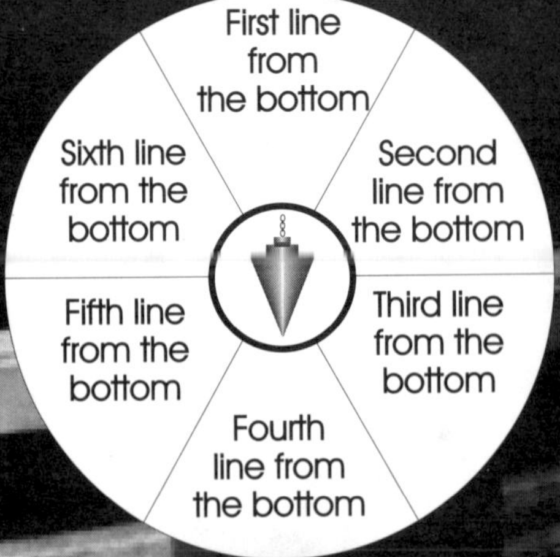

First line from the bottom / Second line from the bottom / Sixth line from the bottom / Third line from the bottom / Fifth line from the bottom / Fourth line from the bottom

Table of the Signs of the Zodiac for Determining the Ascendant

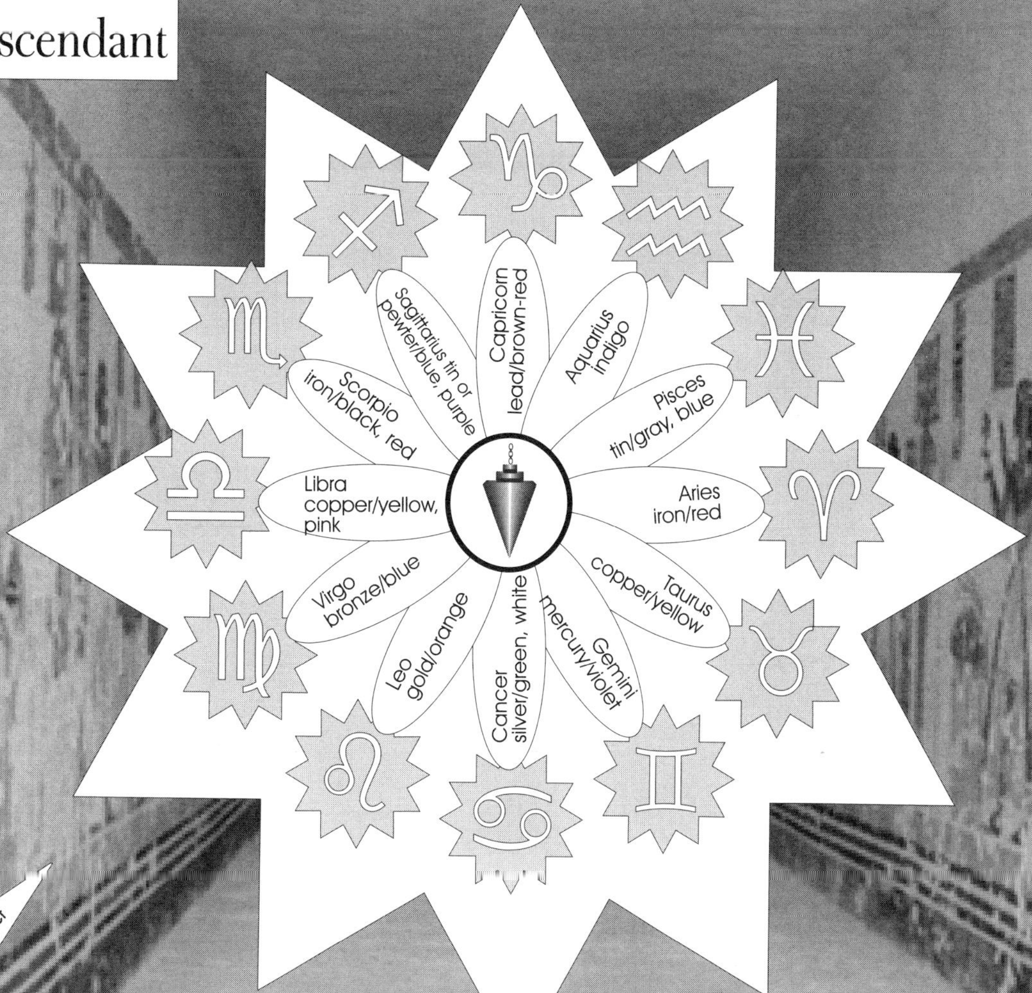

Capricorn
lead/brown-red

Sagittarius tin or
pewter/blue purple

Aquarius
indigo

Scorpio
iron/black, red

Pisces
tin/gray, blue

Libra
copper/yellow,
pink

Aries
iron/red

Virgo
bronze/blue

Taurus
copper/yellow

Leo
gold/orange

Gemini
mercury/violet

Cancer
silver/green, white

This pendulum clock is here to help determine the precise time of your birth. It is divided into segments of 10 minutes each.

Pendulum

22 23 24 1 2
21 3
20 4
19 5
18 6
17 7
16 8
15 9
14 10
13 12 11

Control Table

Correct

Wishful
Thinking

Incorrect

87

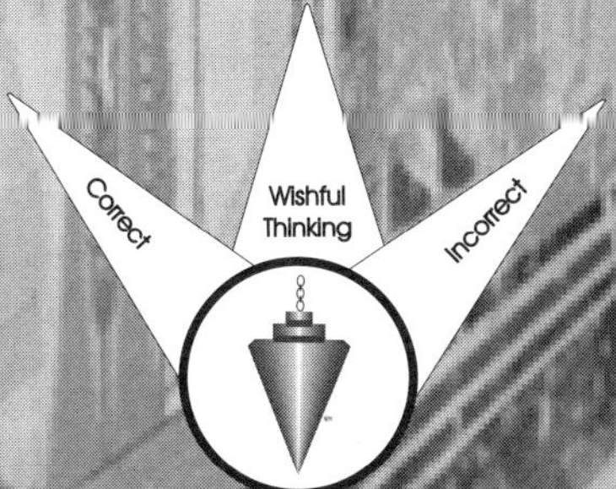

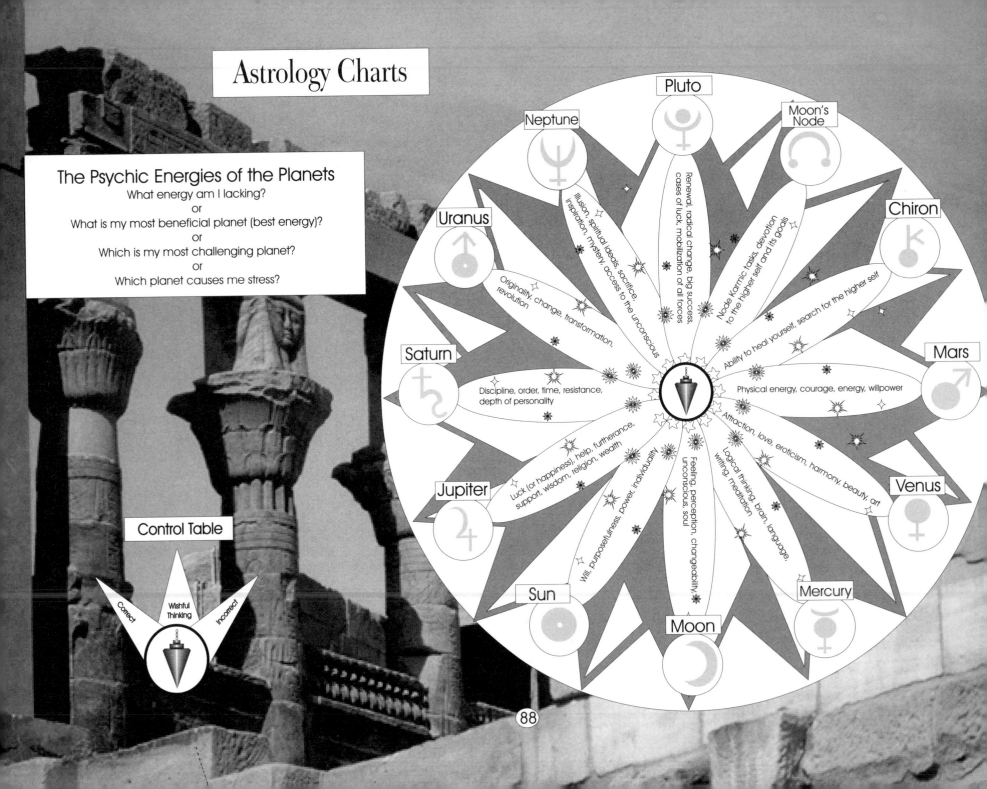

Astrology Charts

The Psychic Energies of the Planets

What energy am I lacking?

or

What is my most beneficial planet (best energy)?

or

Which is my most challenging planet?

or

Which planet causes me stress?

Control Table

Correct — Wishful Thinking — Incorrect

Neptune — Illusion, spiritual ideals, sacrifice, inspiration, mystery, access to the unconscious

Pluto — Renewal, radical change, big success, cases of luck, mobilization of all forces

Moon's Node — Node Karmic tasks, devotion to the higher self and its goals

Chiron — Ability to heal yourself, search for the higher self

Uranus — Originality, change, transformation, revolution

Mars — Physical energy, courage, energy, willpower

Saturn — Discipline, order, time, resistance, depth of personality

Venus — Attraction, love, eroticism, harmony, beauty, art

Jupiter — Luck (or happiness), help, furtherance, support, wisdom, religion, wealth

Mercury — Logical thinking, brain, language, writing, meditation

Sun — Will, purposefulness, power, individuality

Moon — Feeling, perception, changeability, unconscious, soul

Astrology Charts

Evaluation of Houses for Unconscious Blockages and Problems

First, test to see where your blockages lie. Activate your abilities in this area, which are still lying dormant, in order to balance yourself. From time to time, use this chart to check your progress.

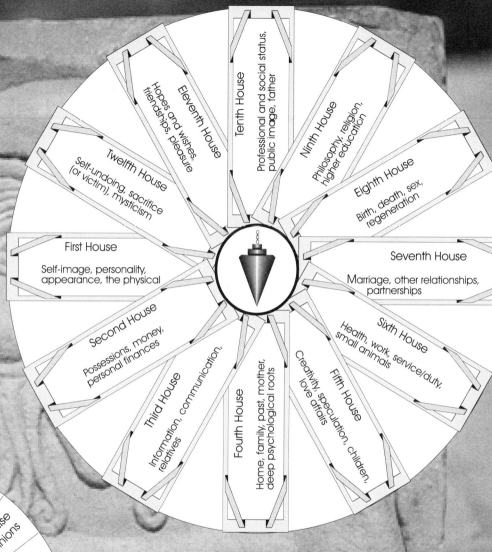

Tenth House — Professional and social status, public image, father

Eleventh House — Hopes and wishes, friendships, pleasure

Ninth House — Philosophy, religion, higher education

Twelfth House — Self-undoing, sacrifice (or victim), mysticism

Eighth House — Birth, death, sex, regeneration

First House — Self-image, personality, appearance, the physical

Seventh House — Marriage, other relationships, partnerships

Second House — Possessions, money, personal finances

Sixth House — Health, work, service/duty, small animals

Third House — Information, communication, relatives

Fifth House — Creativity, speculation, children, love affairs

Fourth House — Home, family, past, mother, deep psychological roots

Control Table

Correct · Wishful Thinking · Incorrect

Why Do I Have this Blockage?

Fear of consequences

Painful experiences

Dishonest with self

Disappointment is expected

Flight into daydreams

False opinions

Bad experiences

Lacking energy

Prejudice

Lacking ability to persevere

Tarot Tables

What is my card of the day?
or
What card will give me protection?
or
What card will lead me to companionship?

Large Arcana   Small Arcana

Control Table

Correct   Wishful Thinking   Incorrect

The Major Arcana

- 0 The Fool
- 1 The Magician
- 2 The High Priestess
- 3 The Empress
- 4 The Emperor
- 5 The High Priest
- 6 The Lovers
- 7 Victory
- 8 Force/Strength
- 9 The Hermit
- 10 The Wheel of Fortune
- 11 Justice
- 12 The Hanged Person
- 13 Death
- 14 Modesty
- 15 The Devil
- 16 The Tower
- 17 The Star
- 18 The Moon
- 19 The Sun
- 20 The Judgment
- 21 The World

Tarot Tables

The Minor Arcana

On which table will
I find my card?

Rods   Cups

Coins   Swords

Control Table

Correct   Wishful Thinking   Incorrect

91

Rod 3, Rod 4, Rod 5, Rod 6, Rod 7, Rod 2, Rod Ace, Rod 8, Rod King, Rod 9, Rod Queen, Rod Knight, Rod Page, Rod 10

Cups 3, Cups 4, Cups 5, Cups 6, Cups 2, Cups 7, Cups Ace, Cups 8, Cups King, Cups 9, Cups Queen, Cups Knight, Cups Page, Cups 10

Coin 3, Coin 4, Coin 5, Coin 6, Coin 2, Coin 7, Coin Ace, Coin 8, Coin King, Coin 9, Coin Queen, Coin Knight, Coin Page, Coin 10

Swords 4, Swords 5, Swords 3, Swords 6, Swords 2, Swords 7, Swords Ace, Swords 8, Swords King, Swords 9, Swords Queen, Swords Knight, Swords Page, Swords 10

Final Remarks

After you have worked your way through many of these diagrams, I'd like to send you on your way with a few thoughts—especially in order to eliminate the reproach that I simplified matters. Here, as in other spiritual matters, the path is the goal!

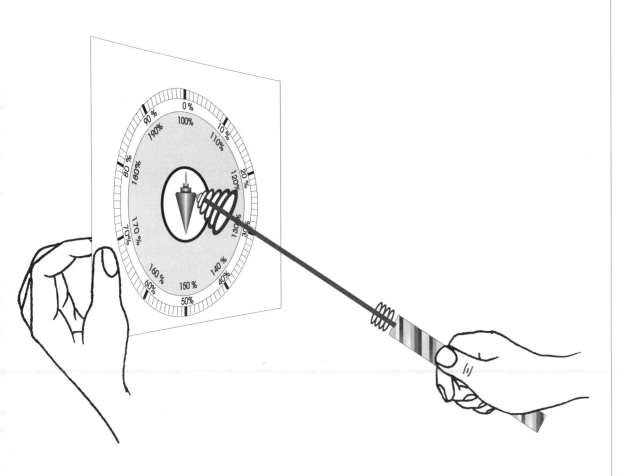

1. Naturally, many things we ask about with the pendulum can also be answered by other means—with a dowsing rod, for example. Which subject you ask about with a pendulum and which you ask about with a rod is, in part, a question of habit. If in doubt, select the tool or method you can deal with best, the one you like best. Remember that pendulums and rods are only enhancers, which show the results of the swing.

2. This book should not give the impression that you have to use charts in order to work with a pendulum. There is a whole world of pendulum swinging besides the one that is presented to you here. But there are reasons for using these charts: first of all, they save you time because you can eliminate many possibilities rapidly, and zero in on the ones that are important for you, or for the person you're reading for. Second, it gives you a wide range of choices—more than you might come up with on your own. Third, the charts make up for gaps in our memory. They save many things from being forgotten, put them in order, and sort them out. How else could you remember all the Bach Flower Remedies by heart? Or many of the essential oils or gemstones? That's why so many charts are presented in this book that have never been published before in this way. They make your work easier.

3. Since sufficient literature exists on all the subjects represented in this book, we have not gone into detail about them. Often you will not need additional information in order to get an answer

from the pendulum. But it is important to remember that your pendulum results may not be perfect, and to use its recommendations only as a guide. Always check with your doctor before taking any of the substances listed internally.

4. For reasons of completeness, I want to mention the possibility of an entirely different type of questioning. While the pendulum can be used to determine almost everything using these charts, sometimes, for practical reasons, a question cannot be answered in this way. The next step, after asking about circumstances via the chart, is mental questioning. Whether you are able to do this or not is, on one hand, a matter of getting thoroughly acquainted with the situation, and, on the other hand, of increasing your sensitivity.

Let's look at a simple example of this mental work.

Exercise 1. Take an apple in your left hand and hold the pendulum between your body and the apple. The question that is going to be asked is: Is this apple good for me? Shall I eat it? You will receive a result depending on the quality of the apple and your physical condition.

Exercise 2. Bring in a second person who takes the apple in his right hand. Hold his right hand with your left. Now the procedure is the same as before. The result should be the same as in Exercise 1.

Exercise 3. Now bring in a third person. Go through the same procedure, and again, you will come up with the same result. You can increase the number of people whom you bring in as much as you want, but the results will always be the same.

All this is still resonance questioning. The steps to mental work follow.

Exercise 4. Place the apple on a table or a chair, etc., far away, but so that you can still see it. Concentrate on the apple. Extend your left hand in order to pick up psychically the swinging of the apple. Ask the same question as in Exercise 1. The result will be the same as in the previous steps.

Exercise 5. Place the apple in the room next door and concentrate on the apple. Meanwhile, make sure you look at the apple long enough and strong enough. Come to know the apple. Ask again: Is the apple on the table next door good for me? Also, in this case, you must get the same result.

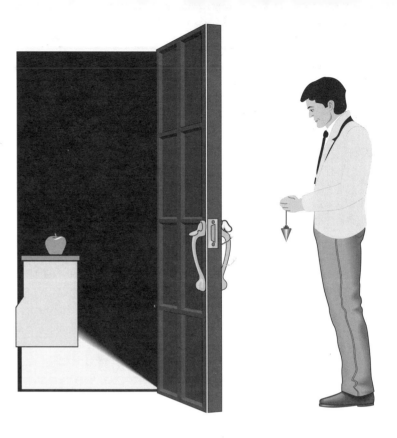

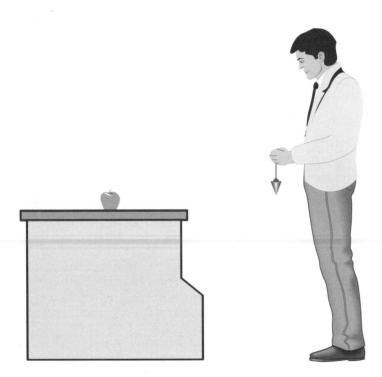

If you do, then you have passed the test. You are able to work mentally as well as with the pendulum. With this ability, worlds up to now unthought of open up for you! Carry on! I wish you continued fun and success!

Index